Contents

Figures

The Great Knob
Interpretations of Monks Mound

Mikels Skele

Illinois Historic Preservation Agency
Springfield, Illinois

International Standard Book Number 0-942579-03-8

Illinois Historic Preservation Agency, Springfield, Illinois 62701
Printed by the authority of the State of Illinois
September 1988

This publication was financed in part with federal funds provided by
the U.S. Department of the Interior and administered by the Illinois
Historic Preservation Agency. However, the contents and opinions do
not necessarily reflect the views or policies of the U.S. Department
of the Interior or the Illinois Historic Preservation Agency.

THE ILLINOIS HISTORIC PRESERVATION AGENCY IS AN EQUAL
OPPORTUNITY EMPLOYER

FIGURES

Acknowledgements

I wish to gratefully acknowledge all those who have helped make this study a reality. My thanks to John Mathes and Associates, the Illinois Historic Preservation Agency, and the Contract Archaeology Program at Southern Illinois University at Edwardsville (SIUE) for the time and space for the greater part of the project. The Lovejoy Library at SIUE contains archives that are unparalleled in the area for local and regional history; my thanks to Louisa Bowen for her help in guiding me through those treasures.

Several institutions and individuals have granted permission to reproduce graphic material for this book. I offer my gratitude to the Archaeological Research Laboratory at the University of Wisconsin-Milwaukee for Figures 31, 33, 38, 44, 46 and 48; the Society for American Archaeology for Figure 51; The Cahokia Mounds State Historic Site for Figures 18, 19, 35, 36, 37 and 42; and the Missouri Historical Society for Figure 32 and the permission to photograph the Patrick model of Monks Mound. The Joslyn Art Museum, Omaha, Nebraska, gave permission and provided excellent prints for figures 10 and 11, and the Illinois State Museum provided the cover illustration. Mark Johnsey took the excellent air photographs for Figures 20, 22, 24 and 26.

My special thanks to Melvin L. Fowler of the University of Wisconsin-Milwaukee, without whose generosity in giving me access to his archives this would have been a rather different paper. Thanks also to William Woods, William Baker and Noble Thompson, members of my thesis committee at SIUE, whose comments and suggestions were helpful and insightful, and to the many people who reviewed this manuscript. Among them were Charles Bareis, Nelson Reed, David Browman, Glen Freimuth, Lawrence Conrad, John Kelly, Edwin Hajic, Charles McGimsey, Michael Wiant, Leonard Blake and Gregory Perino. Chief Archaeologist Thomas Emerson of the Illinois Historic Preservation Agency also reviewed the manuscript and provided many instructive suggestions, and Editor Evelyn Moore of that same agency took an ordinary thesis and deftly and painlessly turned it into a book manuscript.

Last, but certainly not least, I would like to dedicate this book to my wife, Peg. Thanks for your love and encouragement.

Chapter 1. Introduction

In southern Madison County, Illinois, amid a group of more than one hundred prehistoric earthen mounds in and around the Cahokia Mounds State Historic Site, stands the largest such earthwork in the New World, known since the early nineteenth century as Cahokia Mound, or, increasingly over the decades, as Monks Mound, after a small band of Trappists who settled briefly in its shadow. Before that, when it was called anything, it was simply "the Great Knob."

Descriptions of this pile of earth have varied considerably over the two centuries for which we have records. If there is a common thread that runs through them all, it is this: Monks Mound bears explanation. Although its human origin has long been settled, this was not always so. Even recent descriptions and interpretations have suffered from the influence of preconceived notions of its function in prehistoric times. Surprisingly, despite the importance of the physical appearance of Monks Mound in the attempt to understand its function, no rigorous study has been made of its changing characteristics since European contact, with the possible exception of the work of Warren K. Moorehead in the 1920s and 30s. Moorehead compiled a great deal of data concerning the history of the mound, but stopped short of a careful analysis of its reliability. The question remains: has Monks Mound deteriorated to its present configuration from some pristine geometric perfection, or did it always look more or less as it does today? Indeed, what precisely is its present shape?

The dimensions of Monks Mound have been estimated at various figures over the years, depending on where the base of the mound is defined. Fowler (n.d.) gives two sets of figures, one measured from the 130 meter contour line and one from the 128 meter line. All elevations are given as meters above mean sea level. The first is the apparent base, judging from the 1966 University of Wisconsin-Milwaukee (UW-M) photogrammetric contour map, and the second is nearer to the archaeologically defined base of approximately 127.75 (Reed, Bennett and Porter 1968; and McGimsey and Wiant 1984). Thus, taking the horizontal dimensions from the 130 meter contour and the vertical dimensions from the 128 meter contour, we can arrive at a fair approximation. The base is about 291 meters north-south by about 236 meters east-west, roughly rectangular in shape. From this base, the mound rises to its summit in four relatively flat "terraces", conventionally designated as the first through the fourth terraces, numbered from the lowest to the highest (Figure 1).

The first terrace is an apron of about 40 meters in width spanning the south face of the mound, at an average elevation of somewhat less than 140 meters. A ramp descends southward to the plain below from this terrace, slightly offset to the east of center with respect to the first terrace, but roughly on line with the centers of the third and fourth terraces. There is a small rise in the southwest corner of the first terrace where a secondary mound was located.

The second terrace is the least regular of the four; it presently extends approximately 30 meters east-west along the west face of the mound and about 60 meters north of its interface with the first terrace. It is more strongly sloping than the other terraces and has an average elevation of 149 meters. There has been much controversy concerning the original shape and extent of this terrace, and this topic will be discussed more thoroughly in later chapters. Near the top of an extensive gully at the north central portion of the terrace are the remains of a well dug in the 1830s by T. Ames Hill, an early owner of the mound. Hill's access road to the summit bisects the second terrace.

The third terrace is about 50 meters north-south and 40 meters east-west, with an average elevation of 157 meters. Immediately to its north lies the fourth terrace, with somewhat larger dimensions. Its average elevation of 158 meters makes the overall height of Monks Mound about 30 meters.

This feature has stood for nearly a thousand years, and is so firmly fixed in the surrounding topography that many early scholars were convinced that it was a natural remnant of eroded terrace.

In documenting the evolving morphology of Monks Mound, vastly different kinds of material had to be considered. In addition to the body of technical data generated by current and previous archaeological investigations of the mound, itself exhibiting varying degrees of refinement, there were the written accounts of visitors to the mound. These ranged in style and attention to detail from the casual impressions of the tourist to the meticulous observations of the traveling scientist. Graphic representations of Monks Mound also had to be considered; there, too, the degree of reliability ran the gamut from the absurd to the technically faultless.

All of these sources had to be not only compiled, but evaluated. Often, comparisons had to be made between widely different kinds of evidence. In this pursuit, naturally, there is great latitude for interpretation. The present study is offered as a focus for discussion of the various possibilities.

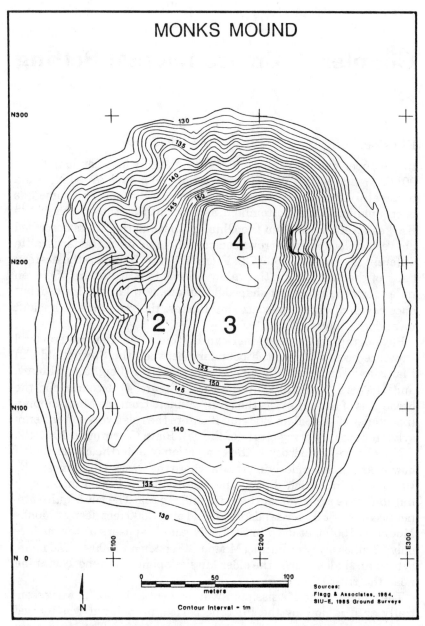

Figure 1. Map of Monks Mound showing the four "terraces"

Chapter 2. Environmental Setting

Physiography

In the upper-middle Mississippi Valley, roughly between longitudes 90° 02'W and 90° 15'W and latitudes 38° 30'N and 38° 54'N, lies a broad alluvial plain known as the American Bottom. The name has been applied to the bottomland as far south as the mouth of the Kaskaskia River, or even the Ohio, but beyond the limits described above, the floodplain narrows considerably and its character is quite different (Fenneman 1909:73). From Alton to Dupo, on the eastern bank of the Mississippi, the valley widens to a maximum of eleven miles, forming a crescent-shaped floodplain, now largely drained, but once covered with numerous small lakes, the remnants of ancient meanders (Figures 2 and 3).

Physiographically, the American Bottom of the Central Lowland Province occurs just at the boundary between the Springfield Till Plains and the Salem Plateau west of the river (Leighton, Ekblaw, and Horberg 1948:18). This location (Figure 4) accounts for the broadness of the valley: as the river wanders from the Mississippian limestones of the Salem Plateau, it enters the relatively softer Pennsylvanian coal-bearing strata of the Till Plain (Yarbrough 1974:12).

The change in bedrock is the expression of a northeastwardly tilt downward in the underlying strata where the Ozark Uplift meets the Illinois Basin, which during the Mississippian Period (about 345 million years ago), was the bed of a shifting sea. The tilt is quite pronounced; the St. Peter sandstone found over 2000 feet deep at Monks Mound is 1500 feet deep in St. Louis, and it appears at the surface only 33 miles away at Pacific, Missouri (Fenneman 1909:4). The Pennsylvanian shales overlie the older Mississippian limestone, beginning near the river (Figure 5).

The trough of the Mississippi River, evident in Figure 5, was essentially as it is now by the Pliocene period; probably it was formed during the late Cretaceous or early Tertiary period. The Mississippi underwent successive episodes of filling and erosion during the Pleistocene glaciations. The nomenclature of these glacial periods is currently undergoing revision (see, for example, Boellstorff 1978); to avoid confusion, the term "pre-Illinoian" is used rather than

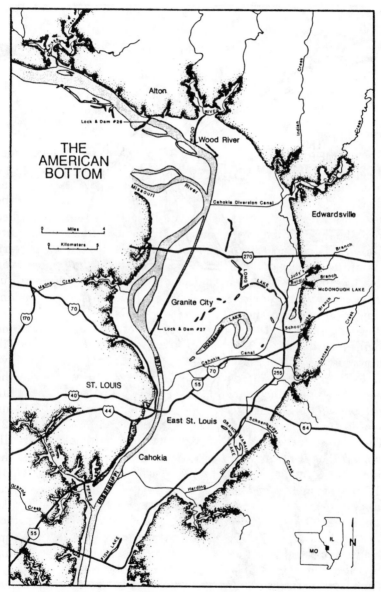

Figure 2. Map of the American Bottom ca. 1987

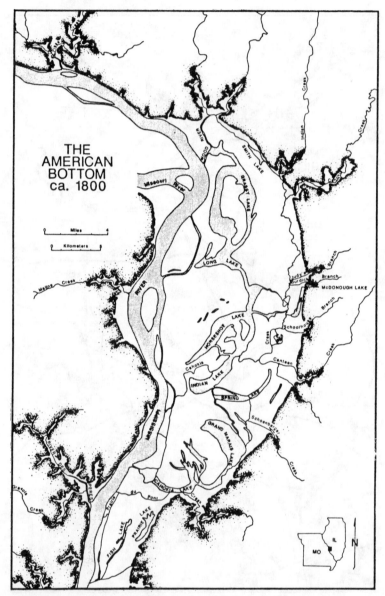

Figure 3. Map of the American Bottom before extensive
drainage systems were built.

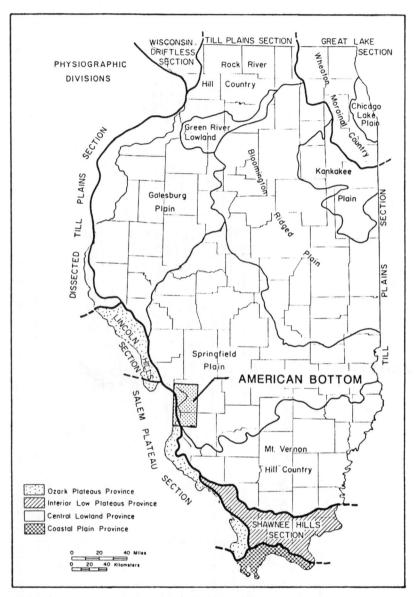

Figure 4. The physiographic context of the American Bottom
(adapted from Willman et al. 1975)

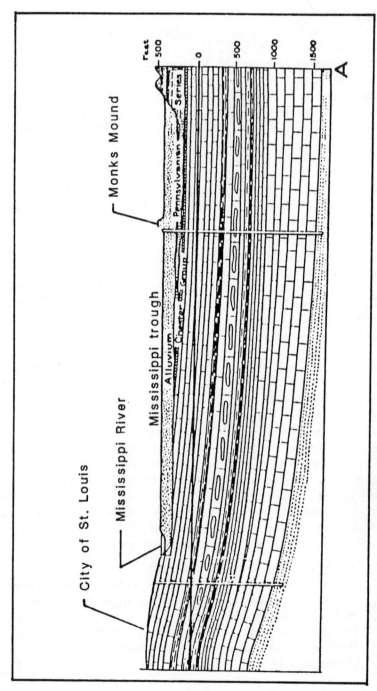

Figure 5. Cross-section of the American Bottom through Monks Mound (adapted from Fennemen 1909)

"Kansan" and "Nebraskan," which are now regarded unfavorably (Edwin Hajic, personal communication).

Representation of the pre-Illinoian glacial stages (preceding about 300,000 years ago) is not well known in this area, although some evidence exists that the leading edge of the pre-Illinoian ice was somewhere near the American Bottom (Frye and Willman 1975:216-219). The first substantial contribution to the fill of the Mississippi Valley at this location was by the Liman substage of the Illinoian glacier, which covered the area from the northeast, terminating across the river in St. Louis County. It contributed deposits of till and some outwash from ponding higher up on the Illinois River.

However, it was during the Wisconsinan, from 75,000 to 10,000 years ago, that the basin was filled in to its present extent. Although the Wisconsinan glaciers terminated less than a hundred miles from the American Bottom, the outwash, carried by the Illinois, the Missouri, and the Mississippi rivers and smaller streams, caused the river valley to aggrade until it reached a level of about 445 feet in elevation, 47 feet higher than present flood basins (Yarbrough 1974:16). During the Wisconsinan winters, prevailing westerly winds swept across the silty alluvium in the bottom and deposited these materials on the eastern bluffs as a cover of loess, up to 50 feet thick in places. When the Wisconsinan glaciers receded, the valley fill degraded and was partially replaced by the alluvium of more recent times.

The present fill of the valley can be divided into two formations: the Henry of the Wisconsinan and the Cahokia Alluvium of the late Wisconsinan and Holocene (Willman and Frye 1970). The Henry Formation, composed mainly of sand and gravel, is found overlying bedrock through most of the bottom, coming to the surface in the northern terrace remnants. Above the Henry, the Cahokia Alluvium is composed mainly of finer silts and clays along with some sands from the Henry Formation. The thickness of the Cahokia Alluvium varies in accordance with the degree of erosion on the underlying Henry. Statigraphically, this recent alluvium is

> poorly sorted as to particle size, although the most
> common cross-section consists of an upper strata of silt
> or clay with interbedded layers of sand, silts, and clays
> below. The silts and a portion of the clays on the sur-
> face probably result from slack water settlement from
> flooding as the channel migrated to another position
> (Yarbrough 1974:16).

The sharpness of the bluff edges is further lessened by valley margin colluvium and the alluvial fans of the smaller tributaries. These alluvial fans are often substantial. As the streams leave their deeply dissected and confined courses in the bluffs and enter the relatively open floodplain, they lose the power to carry their loads of silt and other alluvial materials, and deposit them at the base of the bluffs. These fans often extend for a mile or more into the bottomland and form, along with colluvium from the face of the bluff, a gently sloping plane between the bluff and bottomland. There is some evidence that the rate of this upland erosion was increased by the deforestation activities of the Emergent Mississippian through Mississippian occupants of the bottom (William I. Woods, personal communication).

The picture that emerges, then, is that of a relatively old river trough scoured from the soft Pennsylvanian shales at the edge of the Springfield Plain and filled in with a combination of glacial drift and alluvial material, all of which has been subject to the cut-and-fill activities of the water and weather. The whole has been subdivided into environmentally distinct regions by Yarbrough (1974:18) (Figure 6). The region of interest to us is the part of the Lake Region north of the East St. Louis Rise. This area contains Horseshoe Lake and numerous small lakes and ponds, along with more or less permanent swamps, occupying cut-off meanders of the Mississippi. The soil types are varied; alternating areas of sand and dark clay occur, in accordance with the forms of the old meanders of the river. Within or at short distances from this region could be found fish, waterfowl, small and large game, a variety of wild edible plants, and soil well-suited to horticultural activities. Ceramic clays could also be found, as well as, until fairly recently, timber. Here, east-southeast of Horseshoe Lake, and straddling the confluence of the Cahokia and Canteen creeks, are situated the Cahokia Mounds.

Cultural Setting

Although there are mound complexes elsewhere in the American Bottom, the position of the Cahokia Mounds is clearly nodal relative to the other major mound groups and the waterways in existence at the time of their occupation. Figure 7 is a representation of the distribution of the major Mississippian mound groups in the American Bottom in relation to the configuration of lakes and streams in the region. The map reconstructs the floodplain as it may have appeared around A. D. 1800, before the immense system of levees and drainage canals was developed and the Mississippi channelized, giving a glimpse of what conditions may have been during the Mississippian tenure at Cahokia.

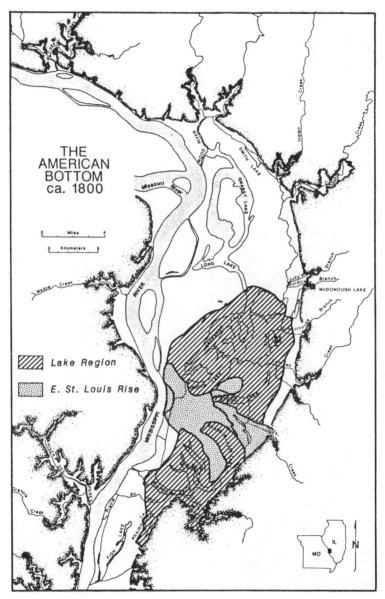

Figure 6. The Lake Region of the American Bottom (after
Yarbrough 1974)

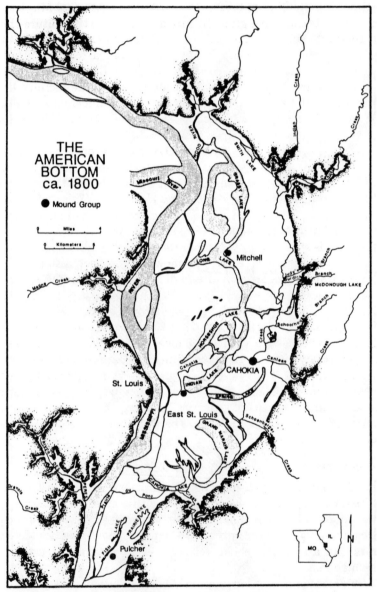

Figure 7. Map of the American Bottom showing the
locations of the major mound groups.

"Mississippian" (not to be confused with the geological Mississippian Period) is the name given by archaeologists to the culture that built the large substructure mounds in the complexes shown on the map. There is no evidence other than archaeological for this culture; they had long since disappeared when the first Europeans arrived. The Cahokia and Tamaroa Indians then living in the vicinity had no knowledge of the origin of the mounds, although George Rogers Clark reported that the Kaskaskias considered the builders of the mounds their ancestors (James 1928:495-499).

Archaeologists have, however, reconstructed a chronology of phases through which the Mississippian culture passed, based on archaeological stratigraphy, scientific dating methods, and the evidence of the materials left behind (Fowler and Hall 1972). This chronology has been refined and supplemented through the recent intensive work on the F.A.I. 270 Archaeological Project and other work in the area. Although it is still subject to further refinement, a workable consensus has been achieved. Figure 8 shows a representation of this chronology at Monks Mound, although it should be pointed out that not all archaeologists would agree with the beginning dates of the earlier stages (Charles Bareis, personal communication).

The sequence chronicles the ascendency, spread, and decline of a culture that reached a near state-level of organization. It was a stratified society with a complex and far-reaching system of trade and religious influence. The material culture was characterized by well-crafted implements of stone, bone, and occasionally copper, a highly refined ceramic tradition, and, of course, the construction of monumental earthen mounds as substructures for residences and ceremonial surfaces.

Ontogenesis

Monks Mound takes the central position among the Cahokia Mounds. The history of European association with this massive construction is recounted in Chapter 3, but it is appropriate here to discuss the long controversy, resolved only in this century, about whether Monks, as well as all of the other mounds, is a natural or artificial phenomenon.

Early accounts took it for granted that the mounds were artificial. The first apparent assertion of any authority that they were not is in A.H. Worthen's classic *Geological Survey of Illinois*:

> ...we infer that these mounds are not artificial elevations, raised by the aboriginal inhabitants of the country, as has been assumed by antiquaries generally, but, on the contrary, they are simply outliers of loess and

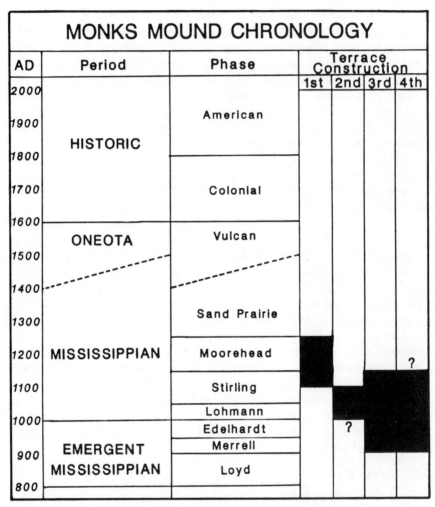

Figure 8. Monks Mound chronology

drift, that have remained as originally deposited, while
the surrounding contemporaneous strata were swept
away by denuding forces (Worthen 1866:314).

The area's geological history, it must be stressed, was not well
understood at the time. In fact, Worthen's work was the first such
study in the area, and some of his conclusions that seem ludicrous
now, made some sense at the time. It is easy to see, however, how
incorrect ideas can reinforce one another. Worthen believed, for example, that the loess formations on the bluffs were water-laid and
once covered the entire plain at nearly the level of the uplands. As
corroboration for this theory, he pointed to the mounds in the
bottomland.

Worthen's assertion that the mounds are composed of the same
materials as the bluffs, and the half-century of acceptance of it as
fact by the geological community, is a little easier to understand when
viewed against the relative lack of data then available. For example, as late as 1907, in Bowman's otherwise excellent and extremely
helpful review of the groundwater resources of the East St. Louis
District, a well cross-section near Monks Mound labels the top 40 feet
of stratification as "dirt" (Bowman 1907:106). Yet one cannot help
but wonder how the clear evidence from Hill's well through a good
portion of Monks Mound could have been so universally ignored. Even
Fenneman, who deserves more credit than usually is attributed to
him with regard to the realization of the artificial nature of the
mound, asserts that "sand is found neatly inter-stratified with loam
at. . .35 feet above its base. To this height, at least, the mound is
natural" (Fenneman 1909:63). He further states that the artificial
character of the mound above this level is evident. It is not clear where
Fenneman found the evidence that he refers to for the natural
stratification up to 35 feet. Possibly a substantial portion of the northwest corner was removed at about the time Fenneman was writing
(see Chapter 4), but there is no conclusive evidence for this.

Other writers, by either poor scholarship or ambiguous references,
perpetuated the notion of the natural origin of the mounds, as in the
case of one 1911 study:

> The occasional bit of terrace such as at Monks Mound
> near St. Louis, 40 feet above the flood plain, which cor-
> responds closely in altitude, and in places connects
> with the fills on the tributaries, indicates that the
> valley floor was formerly 40 feet above the present one
> (Shaw 1911:151).

The convention among geologists of the day that the mounds in the

American Bottom were not artificial, or at least not entirely so, accounts in part for the otherwise puzzling persistence of that notion. Even after 1921, when A.R. Crook and M.M. Leighton, on opposing sides of the argument, witnessed Moorehead's profiling of James Ramey Mound and appeared to settle for all time that the mounds were not natural formations, the matter was not laid to rest. Their reluctance to abandon the idea appears to be grounded more in the culture of the observers than in the data (see discussion in Chapter 3).

Chapter 3.
Historical Background

Early References

Historical references to the Cahokia Mounds in general, and to Monks Mound in particular, appear surprisingly late. The works of such early French writers as Louis Hennepin (1698), a cleric attached to the La Salle expedition, are rife with details of Indian life and customs. He included descriptions of large settlements along the Illinois River and of Tamaroa settlements on the west bank of the Mississippi near the confluence of the two rivers, but not a word about the immense earthworks in the American Bottom. The same is true of Tonti's version of the La Salle expedition (Tonti 1704).

By the eighteenth century, the American Bottom was beginning to see more extensive population by French settlers, and the mounds were undoubtedly well-known local landmarks. Yet, there remained a paucity of written descriptions. Between 1735 and 1752, the French had a mission on the first terrace of Monks Mound, and toward the end of the century a canteen was constructed, probably to the south or west of the mound. The location of the mission has been confirmed by archaeological investigations (Walthall and Benchley 1987). Yet, despite the apparent local familiarity with what must have been a prominent feature of the otherwise level prairie, Monks Mound escaped wider fame for some time. General George Collot's 1796 map of the area (Figure 9) shows "Indian ancient tombs" to the southeast of French Cahokia—apparently the Pulcher group (Fowler n.d:11)—but only a rather conspicuous void where the Cahokia Mounds should be.

George Rogers Clark had written about "the works on the Mississippi near the Caw [Cahokia] River . . . one of the largest we know of . . ." (James 1928:497). His description of Monks Mound is as intriguing as it is scant: ". . . the larger was the real palace [;] that the little Mountain we their [sic] saw flung up with a bason [bastion] on the top was a tower that contained part of the guards . . ." (James 1928:497). This was possibly a reference to a small conical mound at the southeast corner of the summit.

Clark's discussion of the Cahokia Mounds appeared in a letter to

Figure 9. The Collot map (Collot 1826)

the editor of *American Museum* magazine, rebutting a theory that the mound complexes scattered throughout the eastern United States were constructed by DeSoto as a defense against hostile Indian attacks. This theory was developed in a series of articles by Noah Webster in *American Museum* between July and September of 1789 and taken up again in June and July of 1790. Although there is no apparent reference to the Cahokia Mounds specifically, there are some tantalizing allusions (see, for example, Webster 1789:136-141).

One of the earliest written references to the mounds is in the field notes for the U.S. government survey of the south line of township 3 north, range 9 west of the third Principal Meridian:

> Moved temp'ry Post Cor. of Sec 33-34 on true line from
> which two large Mounds Bearing [illegible] in the Edge
> of a large Prairie—Twenty four or more of these
> mounds in Sight at one view—one whose Base is near-
> ly 6, acres by Estimation—& 100 Feet in Height—
> Others of Various Sizes from 6, to forty feet in height,
> & Various forms—some Round, some oblong or Rect.
> Angled Parallelograms and others inagular [sic]—All
> covered with Simtoms of ancient Ruins (Messinger
> 1808:76).

By 1809 Trappist monks had settled on a mound directly southwest of Monks Mound, and inadvertantly given it its name. The letters of the monastery's abbot Father Urban Guillet to the Bishop of Quebec, however, make no mention of the mounds themselves. The only information in these letters of direct bearing on this study of Monks Mound is in one dated February 18, 1812, relating the effects of the New Madrid earthquake:

> A great many houses have been badly damaged, but no
> one was killed. The earth opened in many places,
> especially about three miles from our monastery. Only
> sand and water came from the opening. Fortunately,
> our poor cabins of wood and sand can withstand a
> great deal of shaking. . . . Some stone and brick
> houses have had to be abandoned (McDermott
> 1949:317).

Aftershocks of the New Madrid earthquake lasted several months, with some as severe as the initial quake. Whether the earthquakes affected the structure of Monks Mound bears serious consideration.

The first written description of any consequence of Monks Mound is from Henry Marie Brackenridge's 1811 account in the *Missouri*

Gazette:

> My astonishment was inexpressibly excited when I
> came to the foot of the large mound, as it is called. It
> is certainly a most stupendous pile of earth, and were
> it not for the strongest proof, no one would believe it
> the work of hands. It stands within a hundred yards of
> the creek, on the side next to which, it is clothed with
> timber. As near as I could compute, its circumference
> is about 3,300 feet, and about eighty in height. The
> form is nearly oblong from north to south. On the
> south side there is an apron, or terrace, of one hundred
> and fifty feet in breadth, with a projection near the
> middle of it, of about twenty feet, and ten feet wide, af-
> fording a sloping road up the mound. This terrace, is
> partly occupied as a kitchen garden, while the top of
> the mound is sowed in wheat; the area is sufficient to
> draw up a battalion (Brackenridge 1811).

Two years later in a letter to Thomas Jefferson, Brackenridge
expressed astonishment that the "stupendous monument of
antiquity" had gone so long unnoticed, and even more astonishment
that his published descriptions of it in St. Louis newspapers failed
to arouse much interest (Brackenridge 1813:155). A discrepancy worth
noting is that in the Jefferson letter Brackenridge claims to have
stated the height of Monks Mound to have been one hundred feet;
in the *Missouri Gazette* article he clearly estimated it to be eighty
feet high. Whether this apparent contradiction is the result of later,
more careful examination can only be surmised. At any rate, by the
time he wrote his *Views of Louisiana*, he had split the difference, call-
ing the mound ninety feet high (Brackenridge 1814:188). In all of
these later writings, the circumference is given as 800 paces or yards,
not entirely inconsistent with the earlier figure of 3,300 feet.

Concerning the Trappists, Brackenridge states that they had four
or five cabins on another mound nearby, with ten or fifteen smaller
structures scattered on the plain below. Significantly, he notes that
they intended to build on the "terrace of the large mound," but he
does not state that they actually did (Brackenridge 1814:288). Edmund Flagg, writing in 1838, asserts that the Trappists had, in fact,
built "an extensive structure upon the terrace of the principal mound"
(Flagg 1838:170). It is possible that the monks had realized their am-
bition of building on the big mound after Brackenridge had seen it;
however, there are no references until much later to a Trappist
structure there, and those are ambiguous.

In 1813 Father Urban Guillet sold the land containing Monks Mound back to Nicolas Jarrot, from whom he had purchased it, prior to abandoning the monastery and returning to France (Walthall and Benchley 1987:112). By the time Stephen Long saw it in 1823, the mound, in contrast to the orderly aspect it conveyed to Brackenridge, had become "so overgrown with bushes and weeds, interlaced with briars and vines, that we were unable to obtain an accurate account of its dimensions" (Long 1823:120).

The Hill Tenure

In 1831 a mechanic named T. Ames Hill purchased the tract containing the mound, cut a road from the southwest corner to the summit, and built a substantial house with several outbuildings on the third terrace. On the second terrace, he dug a well, which, according to several accounts, revealed clear evidence of human occupation down to the level of the surrounding plain (Flagg 1838:167, Wild 1841:53, DeHass 1869:296-297).

Despite the increased accessibility such activities provided, contemporary accounts seem to be derived from Brackenridge's published descriptions. Peck's 1834 *Gazetteer of Illinois* says on one page that the circumference of the mound is 800 yards and its height is 90 feet, and on another page that its circumference is 600 yards. He also reported that on the south side, about half way down, was an apron of about fifteen feet in width (Peck 1834:55, 290). Peck apparently misread a dimension of fifteen feet given for the width of the south ramp in one of Brackenridge's accounts as the width of the first terrace. We cannot account for the discrepancy in the circumference. Peck also expresses some doubt as to the artificial origin of the mound (Peck 1834:54).

In the same year that Peck wrote about the mound, German artist Karl Bodmer visited the site and sketched his impressions of the mounds. His representation of Monks Mound appears to be very reliable, and it is the first to show Hill's construction at the summit (Figure 10). The view from the east shows this side much as it appears today—even two of the same gullies that can be seen in modern times are apparent—and at least the northernmost of the two east lobes. Hill's house is shown near the south edge of the third terrace with an outhouse and three substantial outbuildings further back. In addition, his is the only early representation which seems to show that the west side of the first terrace was slightly higher than the east (Bodmer 1834).

Another of Bodmer's drawings (Figure 11) overlooks a stream with mounds scattered in the background. The location is difficult to place,

Figure 10. Bodmer's drawing of Monks Mound (Joslyn Art Museum)

Figure 11. Bodmer's drawing of unidentified mounds in the Cahokia group (Joslyn Art Museum)

but if the view is taken to be south from the first terrace of Monks Mound, with Fox and Roundtop mounds at the upper right, it could be compatible with a later account of a moat surrounding the Monks Mound (see Oliver 1843:170).

Latrobe's 1835 account is of some interest. He describes the slopes gullied by rain and waving with grass and brushwood. And he states that the sides were heavily forested, "with a broad apron to the southward, and a second, yet lower, further in advance" (Latrobe 1835:182). Yet when it comes to numbers, we hear the echo of Peck's 600 yard circumference and ninety foot height. Clearly, Latrobe had not measured the mound for himself.

Edmund Flagg, another tourist with a penchant for description, wrote this detailed account of what he saw:

> As it is first beheld, surrounded by the lesser heaps, it is mistaken by the traveller for an elevation of natural origin: as he draws nigh, and at length stands at the base, its stupendous magnitude, its lofty summit, towering above his head and throwing its broad shadow far across the meadow; its slopes, *ploughed with yawning ravines* by the torrents of centuries descending to the plain; its surface and declivities perforated by the habitations of burrowing animals, and carpeted with tangled thickets; the vast size of the aged oaks rearing themselves from its soil (Flagg 1838:159, emphasis added).

And after a lengthy discourse on the geological context of the mound, he added that the observer

> is compelled, however reluctantly, yet without a doubt, to declare that the gigantic pile is incontestibly the WORKMANSHIP OF MAN'S HAND (Flagg 1838:160).

This appears to settle one point at least: that Monks Mound had much the same gullied appearance in 1838 as it has today, the difference just one of degree.

From this point on, a great deal of confusion is caused by the rather liberal borrowing of Monks Mound descriptions, often without citation, from Brackenridge and others. Sometimes they were accompanied by outlandishly distorted visual representations.

When J.C. Wild wrote about Monks Mound in 1841, Hill was well established. Wild's description is fairly reliable, though the numbers leave something to be desired:

> The greater one, or Monks Mound, is in the form of a

parallelogram, and is estimated to be one hundred and twenty-five feet high. Its top is flat and presents an area of about two acres, laid out in a garden, planted with fruit and shade trees, and containing the residence of the proprietor. On the south side of this mound is a terrace, about two hundred and fifty yards long and ninety in width, perfectly level, and elevated about forty five feet above the surface of the prairie (Wild 1841:52).

In this, as in all subsequent descriptions until well into the twentieth century, the first terrace is described as perfectly level, although we know that there was, and still remains, a prominence on the southwest corner.

Wild also stated that in digging the well on the second terrace, Hill encountered bone fragments, chert, and pot-sherds. And in a flight of pure fancy, he likens the mound to a ruined castle: ". . . the terraces, which on this side, rise with considerable regularity above each other, look as if they were intended for armed hosts to parade upon" (Wild 1841:53). The drawing that accompanies this description (Figure 12) shows Monks Mound in relation to Fox and Round-top, as viewed from the east. A large structure, presumably Hill's house, is shown on the third terrace, and another at about the inter-face between third and fourth terraces.

Roughly contemporary with this view was that of G.W. Featherstonhaugh, who visited Hill in 1834-35 and published a description and drawing of Monks Mound in 1844 (Figure 13). His description is noteworthy for the dimensions of the combined third and fourth terraces, given as about 160 feet wide at the north and about 350 feet long on the east side. He notes that the width is less at the south end, but that he has the impression that it once was the equal of the north. He also states that Hill excavated an emminence on the summit of the mound to lay the foundation for his house (Featherstonhaugh 1844:266-268). This is the first specific mention of a smaller mound surmounting the third terrace; his drawing, although representing a badly distorted view of the mound in general, does show what is apparently a reconstruction of the small mound, since it would have already been removed by the time of Featherstonhaugh's visit.

Featherstonhaugh's account is consistent with the present appearance of the third and fourth terraces: the south end of the third terrace is narrower than the north end of the fourth, except for a roundish blip at the southeast corner. It has been suggested that this is where Hill pushed the fill from the small mound over the edge

Figure 12. J.C. Wild's drawing of some of the Cahokia Mounds (Wild 1841)

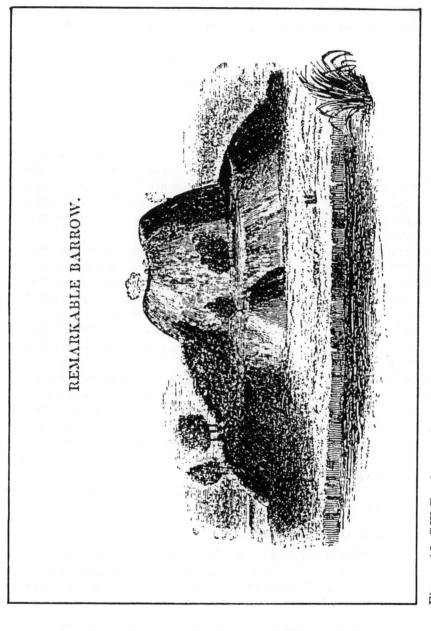

REMARKABLE BARROW.

Figure 13. G.W. Featherstonhaugh's drawing of Monks Mound, showing the possible secondary mound on the third terrace (Featherstonhaugh 1844)

(Fowler n.d.:182).

One observer, William Oliver, reported that a moat surrounded the mound:

> The earth for the construction of this huge mass has
> been lifted from the circumference of its base, as is
> evident from the regular ditch-like depression
> intervening between it and the surface of the prairie
> (Oliver 1843:170).

But he admits that he "could not ride around it for fences and corn fields" (Oliver 1843:170). The only other suggestion of a moat was in Wild's fantasy of Monks Mound as a castle. Still, Oliver's assertion is unambiguous, even to the extent of speculating about how the water may have been drained out of the ditch (see discussion of Bodmer above).

At about the same time, the area's poulation growth warranted a direct road from Collinsville to St. Louis. Madison County road records show that Isaiah Robinson, county surveyor, surveyed two possible rights-of-way past Monks Mound: the first to the north of the mound, roughly where I-55/70 runs today; and the second where US 40 runs today (Figures 14 and 15). The plats are dated 1846 and 1847, respectively, and are for proposed roads (Madison County Road Records Book 2:72,89).

It is not clear whether the more northerly road was built, but the southerly one was. A plank road was constructed soon after the survey, and many years later became US 40. One might assume that since Hill's road up the mound had been cut to provide access from the south, that a path already existed on that side of the mound. It was not until later, however, that it became a publicly maintained right-of-way.

In 1859 Hill died and was buried at the northwest corner of the fourth terrace.

The First Archaeologists

In 1869, Wills DeHass, one of the first archaeologists to examine the mounds, published his views on the subject. Speculation as to the natural or artificial character of the mounds had gained momentum; of proponents of natural origin, the writer says:

> The only charitable conclusion is they never examined
> the mounds. No man whose opinions are worth quoting
> could have examined even one of these interesting
> monuments, and not declared, unequivocally, in favor
> of artificial origin (DeHass 1869:291).

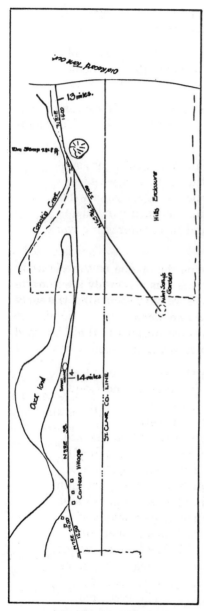

Figure 14. 1846 plat showing a proposed road west of Monks Mound

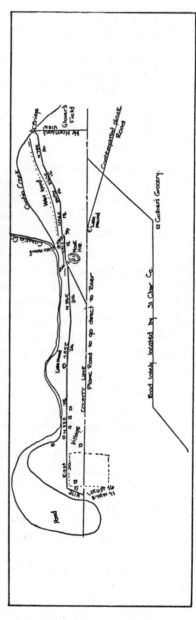

Figure 15. 1847 plat showing proposed road south of Monks Mound

Alluding to his own extensive geological and archaeological investigations in the American Bottom DeHass wrote:

> I have the gratification to know that the question of
> the mounds—whether natural or artificial—has been
> forever settled (DeHass 1869:292).

His assumption was far from the truth, as we shall see further on.
DeHass was also one of the first to decry the "recent" deterioration of Monks Mound:

> It was doubtless originally an immense tetragon, supported by a heavy terrace on the south and west, approached by a talus. The destructive agencies of wind and water, uprooting of trees and modern vandalism have much defaced this vast and most interesting work (DeHass 1869:295).

That impression of destruction was no doubt due to the virtually universal notion that the second terrace was originally coextensive with the west face of the mound. But as we have seen, all of the early accounts describe it as badly gullied and worn.
One of DeHass's more important contributions is the first good overall description of the mound since Brackenridge:

> Its present dimensions are: north base, five hundred
> and sixty feet; south base, seven hundred and twenty
> feet; summit, length, three hundred and ten feet;
> breadth, one hundred and forty six feet.
>   The north side is the most precipitous. The terrace
> approaches from the south and west, and is in depth
> one hundred and twenty feet. The talus approaches
> from the south, is fifty five feet broad at top, one hundred and twenty feet in length, and one hundred and
> twenty-five broad at base. Perpendicular height of
> mound, as nearly as can be ascertained, ninety-one
> feet. It was originally, even within the historic period,
> considerably higher. The base covers nearly six acres.
> The solid contents have been roughly estimated at
> twenty five million cubic feet. . . . The great mound
> was originally surmounted by a conical mound ten feet
> in height (DeHass 1869:296).

This is, of course, not the first mention of the small mound on the third terrace, but is the first to provide a height. Since DeHass interviewed the widow of Hill, the man who removed the mound, it can be taken as reasonably reliable. DeHass also mentions excavations for a cellar, a cistern, and an ice-house, presumably on the third terrace. Concerning the Trappists, he asserts that they did not build on the big mound, but he appears to be relying on Brackenridge (DeHass 1869:297). His contention that the mound had once been much higher is suspect.

In 1864 the tract of land containing Monks Mound was purchased by Thomas J. Ramey, whose heirs owned and lived on the land until it was purchased by the State in 1923. Ramey made several modifications on and near the mound.

He built a brick house at the base of what is now the northernmost spur that radiates from the west face of the mound. Ramey excavated a considerable amount of fill to accomodate the foundation and a small road that rises to the ridge behind. The house was enclosed with a fence, and a large shed was constructed to the west of it, at the feather edge of the mound. The mound itself was surrounded by a fence, and a road ran from the southwest corner at least to the house to the north.

An illustration in the 1873 *Illustrated Encyclopedia and Atlas Map of Madison County, Illinois,* purportedly shows Monks Mound as it then appeared (Figure 16). The brick house in the northwest corner is shown, as well as the road along the west edge and the large shed. The mound is shown moderately timbered, and the Collinsville-St. Louis road runs along the south. Up to that point it seems to be fairly accurate, but there are several apparent anachronisms. The most glaring is the French-style structure shown on the third terrace. We know that Hill's house was in ruins nine years later (McAdams 1882:59), and since Ramey built and occupied the brick house, it is unlikely that the house on the third terrace would still have been in the condition in which it is shown in 1873.

In fact this depiction appears to be essentially a copy of an earlier drawing that appeared as a frontispiece in McAdams (1882) (Figure 17). It is described simply as a "well-known drawing" of the mound. We can surmise that this original drawing dates from before 1850, since it does not show the Collinsville-St. Louis road or any of Ramey's modifications. The 1873 drawing is identical with the exception of these additions. The probability is that, at least in 1873, the structure on top was thought to be the "Monastery of La Trappe."

Both drawings show Hill's well on the second terrace, and its location is significant with respect to the morphology of the second terrace, since it is shown on reasonably level ground. The well exists today, capped with concrete, but it is about a fourth of the way down the side of a deep ravine that runs roughly west-northwest.

In addition to the buildings, fences, and roads, Ramey also dug a

Figure 16. Monks Mound drawing in an 1873 atlas of Madison County, Illinois (Anonymous 1873)

Figure 17. Monks Mound drawing used as a frontispiece in McAdams's 1882 book (1882)

tunnel into the north face of Monks Mound. McAdams describes the
event this way:

> About midway, on the north side, or face of the
> pyramid, and elevated 25 or 30 feet above the base, in
> a small depression, stands a pine tree, singularly
> enough, since this tree is not found in the forrests [sic]
> in this locality. There was a story rife among the early
> settlers that this tree stood at the mouth of an opening
> or gallery into the interior of the mounds. To ascertain
> the truth of this matter, Mr. Thomas Ramey, the pre-
> sent owner of the mound commenced a tunnel at this
> tree and excavated about ninety (90) feet towards the
> centre of the mound. When fifteen feet from the en-
> trance to the tunnel a piece of lead ore was discovered
> but no other object of interest was found (McAdams
> 1882:59).

McAdams's descriptions of the soils found in the various excavations would provide both sides in the natural/artificial controversy,
which DeHass had thought to have settled forever, with arguments
in their favor. The 1873 atlas had pronounced matter-of-factly in favor
of the mounds as natural formations, though conceding that many
thought them artificial. Still, most writers accepted as fact that they
were artificial (Reynolds 1879:148, Short 1880:41-42, and others). The
notable exceptions were the geologists.

The Modern Archaeologists

In 1876 there began a relatively more intensive study of the Cahokia
Mounds by archaeologists and geologists alike. In that year, Dr. John
J.R. Patrick of Belleville commissioned a survey of the entire mounds
area by St. Clair County Surveyor F. G. Hilgard. On the resulting
map, Patrick assigned numbers to each of the mounds; his number-
ing system, augmented by Warren K. Moorehead in the 1920s and
others, is in use today. Patrick's map contained a very good representation of Monks Mound and was supplemented by two cast-iron models
of the mound, one which showed it as it appeared in 1876 and the
other as he thought it had been in antiquity. The map and the models
will be discussed in greater detail in the next chapter.

Patrick's meticulous observations established a new benchmark for
accounts of the mounds and excited a great deal of scholarly interest
as well. In an 1880 report to the Peabody Museum, in which a drawing of one of Patrick's models was included, F.W. Putnam expressed
a hope for further investigation of Monks Mound, ". . . the struc-

ture and object of which cannot be fully understood until a thorough examination has been made" (Putnam and Patrick 1880:14). However, Putnam stressed that the mound should not be destroyed by indiscriminate excavations. The destruction of the Big Mound in St. Louis in 1869 had caused sufficient alarm among scholars to warrant their concern that Monks Mound not share its fate.

About this time rumors purported that Monks Mound was already gone, due perhaps to the confusion of Monks Mound with Big Mound propagated by writers who apparently had never visited the area. In one review of North American antiquities, the writer refers to "the great Mound of Cahokia, which once rose to a height of ninety feet" (Short 1880:41). The rumors persisted for some time; later accounts took the demise of the mound as accomplished (MacLean 1885:42-43, Foster 1887:107) This confusion added to the problem of assuring the preservation of the mound.

After Patrick the next investigator of significance was William McAdams, who left this description:

> The form of the Cahokia Mound is a parallelogram, with straight sides, the longer of which are north and south. It is about one hundred feet in height.
>
> On the southern end, some 30 feet above the base is a terrace or apron, containing near two acres of ground.
>
> On the western side, and some thirty feet above the first terrace is a second one of somewhat less extent.
>
> The top of the mound is flat and divided into two parts, the northern end being some four or five feet higher than the southern portion. The summit contains about an acre and a half.
>
> Near the middle of the first terrace, at the base of the mound, is a projecting point, apparently the remains of a graded pathway to ascend from the plain to the terrace. The west side of the mound below the second terrace, is very irregular and forms projecting knobs, separated by deep ravines, *probably the result of rainstorms*, to the northwest corner of the base of the structure *there seems to be a small mound attached* . . .
>
> The remaining sides of the structure are quite straight and but little defaced by the hand of time (McAdams 1882:58-59, emphasis added).

Two things are apparent in this account. The first is that the gullied appearance of the west side is attributed to erosion, reaffirming the notion that the second terrace originally extended the length of the west side. The second is the mention of a small mound attached to the northwest corner of the mound, the first such mention in any account. No suggestion of such a mound appears on either Patrick's map or his model, although the model clearly shows the northwest corner extending far beyond its present dimensions. Modern topographic maps do show a kind of rise in the northwest corner, but it is unclear whether it is to this that McAdams referred. The discussion of maps and photographs in the next chapter will delve more extensively into this matter.

By McAdams's time, the road running to the south of the mound was, according to a history of St. Clair County, macadamized (Anonymous 1881:61). The date of that improvement is not given. The same source also discusses the flood of 1844, which inundated the American Bottom to the extent that "large steamboats sailed from bluff to bluff. The villages of Cahokia, Prairie du Pont, Prairie du Rocher, and Kaskaskia were almost destroyed" (Anonymous 1881:62). One can only speculate about what effect the flooding may have had on Monks Mound and its surrounding topography.

McAdams did a considerable amount of archaeological investigating at the Cahokia Mounds, and among his accounts of his discoveries is this one:

> In excavating near the base of the great temple mound of Cahokia, whose towering height of over one hundred feet gave a grateful shade for our labors, we found in a crumbling tomb of earth and stone a great number of burial vases, over one hundred of which were quite perfect (McAdams 1887:57).

It is unclear exactly where this excavation was, but one can assume that since the excavators labored in the shade of the mound, that it was somewhere near the north face. Cyrus Thomas locates it at a short distance from the northeast corner, in the lowland (Thomas, 1894:133)

McAdams also surveyed the area of the mounds and made a map, but Monks Mound is poorly represented on it. He gives its dimensions as "about one hundred feet [high], from actual measurement" (McAdams 1887:101), and:

> The longest axis . . . is nine hundred and ninety eight feet, the shortest, seven hundred and twenty one feet; and it covers sixteen acres, two roods, and three perches of ground (McAdams 1887:107).

Stephen Peet, writing in *American Antiquarian* in 1891, reviewed the first-hand descriptions of the mound, relying heavily, as have most other writers, on Brackenridge. In describing the mound, he says:

> In reference to the present condition of the mound, we have to say that an air of waste and ruin surround it; deep gullies are worn into its sides, and it seems to be wrinkled and ridged with the marks of great age. See Plate I (Peet 1891:9).

Plate I, to which Peet referred, showed a nearly perfect second terrace extending the entire length of the west side, with a few minor gashes at its edge. One has to wonder how close Peet got to the mound. He asserts erroneously that "the terraces seem to cut across the whole face of the great pyramid on the south and west sides" (Peet 1891:10). We know from Patrick's fine work fifteen years earlier that this was not so.

At the turn of the century, interest in mounds, both scholarly and popular, was mounting. The World's Fair, which was planned for 1893 at St. Louis, prompted one Harlan Smith to propose excavating the mound for material to exhibit at the fair. After advocating the preservation of the mound as a public park, he continues:

> But there is no warrant to reason from the known contents of the conical burial mounds . . . to the unknown interior of the great pyramid called the Cahokia Mound. . . .
>
> Its contents, which could properly be laid bare only after weeks of patient effort, by hundreds of laborers . . . the secrets of Cahokia Mound, if properly exploited, would constitute an exhibit, at the World's Fair of 1903 (Smith 1902:203).

Fortunately, his recommendations were not followed.

Some idea of the motivations underlying the debate over whether the mounds were artificial or natural is provided by Reverend Henry Mason Baum, who quoted Foster. In listing the reasons why the mound builders could not have been ancestral to the Indians, Foster, after a lengthy disquisition concerning the inferior characteristics of the Indian skull, wrote:

> His character, since first known to the white man, has been signalized by treachery and cruelty. He repels all efforts to raise him from his degraded position; and whilst he has not the moral nature to adopt the virtues of civilization, his brutal instincts lead him to welcome

> its vices. He was never known voluntarily to engage in
> an enterprise requiring methodical labor; . . . To sup-
> pose that such a race threw up the strong lines of cir-
> cumvallation and symmetrical mounds which crown so
> many of our river terraces, is as prepostrous, almost,
> as to suppose that they built the pyramids of Egypt
> (Baum 1903:218).

Such blind racism in the guise of scholarship left one with two alternatives: either the mound builders were a separate, superior, and ex-
tinct race, or the mounds were of natural origin. Of the alternatives,
the second did not seem as unreasonable as the first, although even
McAdams believed that the mound builders were not ancestral to "our
red Indians" (McAdams 1895:304).

Baum contributed to the perpetuation of some misconceptions concerning the topography of the mound as well. He mentions a cistern
on the eastern edge of the summit and the remains of a cellar, both
of which he attributes to the Trappists. He also describes the second
terrace as extending "the entire length of the west side, with deep
ravines cut by rain erosion" (Baum 1903:220). These impressions were
apparently a result of a too-literal reading of Peet.

Baum was, however, an advocate of the preservation of Monks
Mound. In that respect he praises the heirs of Thomas Ramey:

> The sons are religiously guarding it to-day against
> despoilation and, in order to protect it from erosion by
> wind and rain, it has been surrounded by a fence and
> made a pasture for cattle and sheep (Baum 1903:220).

The years 1907-09 saw the return of a more rigorous approach to
the study of Monks Mound. Clark McAdams, the son of William
McAdams, in an address before the Illinois Historical Society, urged
that the mound and, indeed, the entire Cahokia Mounds area be
preserved.

Cyrus Thomas, in a 1909 article, proposed a way in which the
Indians could have erected the mound, based on directly observed
phenomena:

> The method by which they built up these mounds is
> not a mere supposition, as the lumps or small masses
> of earth which formed the individual loads have been
> observed in several instances (Thomas 1907:363).

But Snyder questioned this conclusion by suggesting that at least
part, if not all, of Monks Mound may have been natural, advocating
more study (Snyder 1909:91). In 1917, he threw down the gauntlet

concerning the origin of Monks Mound:

> I have given the result of my examination, some time
> later, of the drift clay excavated from [Ramey's] tun-
> nel. . . . That examination, together with Mr.
> Ramey's account of his excavation, and close inspec-
> tions of the substance of the mound, exposed in its
> many deep gashes and gullies of erosion, led me to
> *believe* that it was originally an outlier of the bluff for-
> mation left there by receding glacial currents, subse-
> quently modeled in geometric proportions by the In-
> dians. But I do not *know* that to be so; nor does anyone
> else. And until the great tumulus is thoroughly ex-
> plored by systematic trenching or tunnelling we cannot
> be positive of the mode of its construction (Snyder
> 1917:259).

This was also basically Fenneman's idea of the mound (see Chapter 2).

It was not until 1928 that Warren K. Moorehead and M.M. Leighton of the University of Illinois took up the challenge. They made three auger borings into Monks Mound and cross- sectioned James Ramey Mound, finally establishing to everyone's satisfation that the mounds were wholly artificial (Moorehead 1928:136-139). Even A.R. Crook, a geologist with the Illinois State Museum who had previously declared them to be unquestionably natural, was convinced:

> The west face [of James Ramey Mound, #3] was
> chimneyed and carefully hand trowelled and minutely
> studied by Dr. M.M. Leighton, Professor of Pleistocene
> Geology at the University of Illinois, and the writer.
> Unusual care was used since Leighton inclines to the
> idea that the mounds are artificial, while the writer
> has regarded them as natural. The deposits had the
> unpleasant tendency of sustaining Leighton's view
> (Crook 1922:5).

Moorehead was a great historian of the Cahokia Mounds, as well as a champion for their preservation as a state park. His references comprise a major resource for the study of the area. His dream of preserving the mounds as a state park had been realized in 1923. In 1930 a museum was built, apparently on the spot formerly occupied by Ramey's house at the turn of the century (Grimm 1949:51).

Despite the meticulous attention to detail by investigators of the mounds since Patrick, a significant amount of misinformation continued to be published, particularly in popular books and journals, though not there alone. Titterington, for example, refers to the small mound surmounting the third terrace of Monks Mound as being in the center of the south face (Titterington 1938:1). This is not surprising given the jumble of contradictory accounts since Brackenridge; where direct evidence could not substantiate a particular assertion, its evaluation was left to the investigator.

Chapter 4.
Maps And Photographs

The Patrick Map and Models

The first reliable cartographic representation of Monks Mound was in a map of the Cahokia Mounds commissioned by Dr. John J. R. Patrick of Belleville in 1876 (Figure 18). The survey for the map was conducted by county surveyor F. G. Hilgard with the help of B.J. Vancourt of O'Fallon and Wm. J. Seever of St. Louis (Moorehead 1922:13). Instead of an idealized or impressionistic view of the mound, their's was an attempt to render it exactly as it stood, as nearly accurate as possible. The technique of shading for the slopes makes it difficult to gauge the grade, but the topography is clearly shown. One can see the two large east lobes with a smaller one between, the steep, ridged north face, and the irregular second terrace. Hill's road is shown rising from the southwest and cutting through the second terrace to the interface between the third and fourth terraces. The summit appears not too different from its modern aspect, and the first terrace with its graded ramp is shown.

Along with the general map of the Cahokia Mounds is a sketch map of Monks Mound alone, apparently showing Hilgard's survey traverse (Figure 19). Graphic detail is lacking; relief is shown with hachures, but only in a general sort of way. Areas and elevations on the terraces are shown, and there are illegible numbers ascending the sides of the mound. Unfortunately, the originals of both of these maps, which are in the Missouri Historical Society collection, are in poor condition. If the numbers on the sides were readable, it might be possible to reconstruct a rough isoline map of the mound for direct comparison with later maps.

However, Patrick's cast-iron model, also in the Missouri Historical Society collection, is in excellent condition. Much can be learned by comparing low oblique photographs of it with air photos taken at roughly the same angles by Mark Johnsey in November 1985.

1. *East Low Oblique (Figures 20 and 21)*: This perspective clearly shows the two main lobes jutting out massively from a rather abrupt east face. Archaeological excavation has suggested that these are the

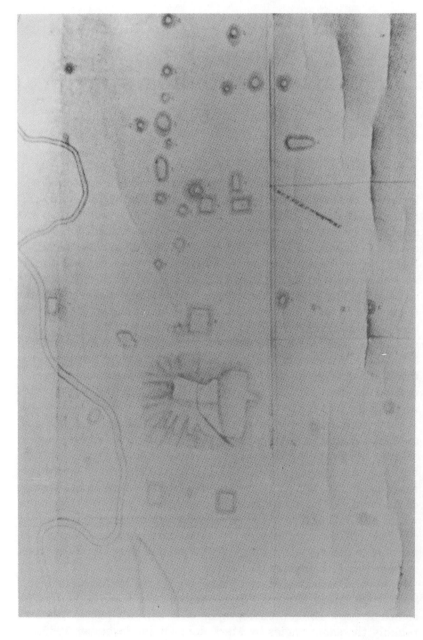

Figure 18. A portion of Patrick's map of the Cahokia Mounds. Photo courtesy Cahokia Mounds State Historic Site

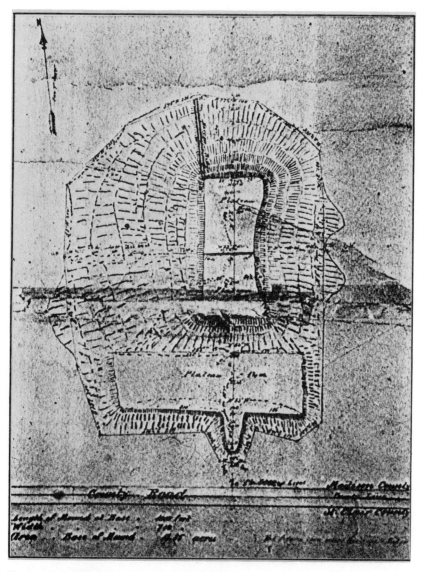

Figure 19. Sketch map of Hilgard's traverse of Monks Mound.
Courtesy Cahokia Mounds State Historic Site

Figure 20. Monks Mound, east low oblique

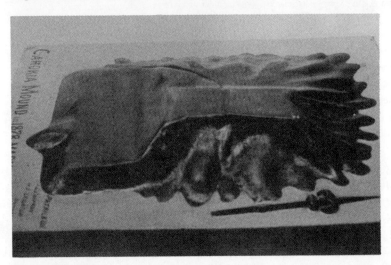

Figure 21. Patrick model, east low oblique

result of prehistoric slumps (Williams n.d.). The Johnsey air photo shows the east face much more uniformly gradual, with the lobes, though easily distinguishable, more integrated into the east face. This may be the result of one hundred years of surface erosion softening the contours. Interestingly, the massive slump on the east face in 1984 left the northernmost lobe looking very much like the Patrick model.

2. North Low Oblique (Figures 22 and 23): This shows the north face with much the same appearance as today. It rises steeply from the plain and is characterized by a series of ridges. Three small indentations are shown at the top feather edge of the fourth terrace; it has been speculated that these may represent slumps in Patrick's time. One startling feature is a very prominent ridge extending from the northwest corner of the fourth terrace, well into the plain below. It is extremely unlikely that this is an error on Patrick's part, given its prominence and the overall attention to detail in other aspects of the model. In the center of the north face is a gully-like indentation; one wonders whether the unconsolidated fill of Ramey's tunnel was the cause of some earlier slumping.

The Johnsey photo shows the prominent ridge on the northwest corner entirely and unequivocally gone. McAdams (1882:59) had referred to a small mound attached to the northwest corner; it is not shown on the Patrick model, nor on the map. A small prominence is, however, apparent today, while the ridge is not. The ridge may have been removed in the intervening eight years, leaving a mound-like pile of dirt; an analysis of early air photos suggests that the road cutting the corner of the mound may have prompted its removal.

3. West Low Oblique (Figures 24 and 25): This provides another view of the ridge on the northwest of the mound, as well as a good view of the second terrace as it appeared in 1876. Roughly the south half of the second terrace appears to be intact, with the exception of where Hill's road cuts through at an angle to the northeast. The north half does not differ greatly, except in degree, from its appearance today. At the base of what is now the northernmost ridge emanating from the west face, the cut for Ramey's brick house can clearly be seen. The Johnsey photo shows a second terrace somewhat eroded, with the gullies a bit more extensive toward the north. The south half of the second terrace looks much the same, except to the west of Hill's road, where a slump occurred in the 1960s. Here, a rather extensive flat section has been reduced to a single spur-like projection.

4. South Low Oblique (Figures 26 and 27): This shows a perfectly flat first terrace, suggesting that errors on the model are likely to be errors of omission. An interesting feature of this perspective is that one can

Figure 22. Monks Mound, north low oblique

Figure 23. Patrick model, north low oblique

Figure 24. Monks Mound, west low oblique

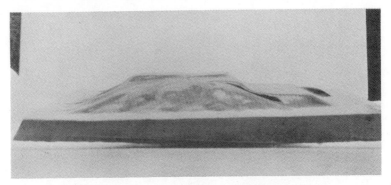

Figure 25. Patrick model, west low oblique

Figure 26. Monks Mound, south low oblique

Figure 27. Patrick model, south low oblique

clearly see a ramp on the south face of the second terrace leading from the first terrace. A view of the south profile of the model gives an even better view of the ramp. In the absence of archaeological evidence, one can only speculate about whether this feature was made in historic or prehistoric times. The Johnsey photo gives no modern evidence of such a ramp. Also, in comparing the model with the air photo, one is also struck by the appearance that the second terrace once extended much further to the west than it does today.

In summary, there are several differences between the Patrick model and the views shown by the Johnsey air photos. Erosion has softened the contours in the intervening century, but there have been no radical changes, with the exception of the disappearance of a prominent ridge running from the northwest corner of the fourth terrace to well beyond the modern gravel road that runs around the north and west perimeters of the mound. In addition, the south half of the second terrace has been diminished considerably, and a ramp that led from the first terrace to the second terrace on its south face can no longer be seen.

Other Early Depictions

After Patrick there are few good representations of Monks Mound until much later. F. W. Putnam of the Peabody Museum contributed to some confusion by producing a drawing of Patrick's model, accurate in most respects, but entirely lacking the very prominent east lobes (Figure 28). The drawing was subsequently reproduced in Moorehead (1928) and elsewhere. Since this drawing appeared in a report co-authored by Patrick (Putnam and Patrick 1880), it was endowed with an authenticity not entirely deserved.

McAdams, in 1882, produced a map of the Cahokia Mounds in general, in which he gives the elevations of the individual mounds, but his drawing of Monks Mound (Figure 29) is, at best, schematic. Although he stated that he completed a thorough survey of Monks Mound, no map of it was published.

Other maps of the Cahokia area from about this time, notably Cyrus Thomas's 1894 map (Figure 30) seem to be derivative of McAdams and show no improvement with respect to Monks Mound. An 1888 Corps of Engineers map shown in Fowler (n.d.) shows the mound as a formless elevation.

In the 1890s, several photographs were made of Monks Mound (Figures 31 through 33). These are extremely valuable because they show the disposition of the buildings, fences, roads, and pathways constructed by the Ramey family. Concerning the ridge at the north-west corner, the photographs are inconclusive, although Figure 32

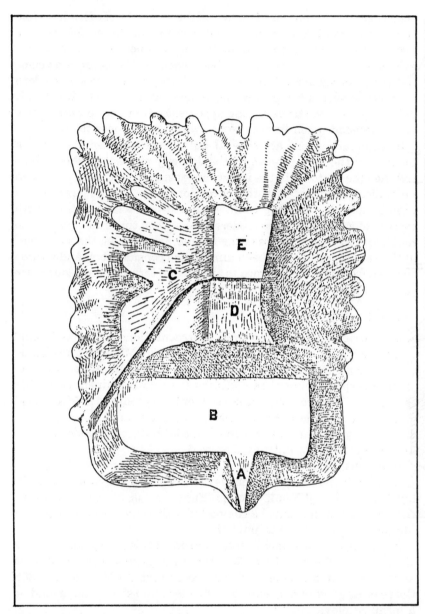

Figure 28. F. W. Putnam's drawing of the Patrick model (Putnam and Patrick 1880)

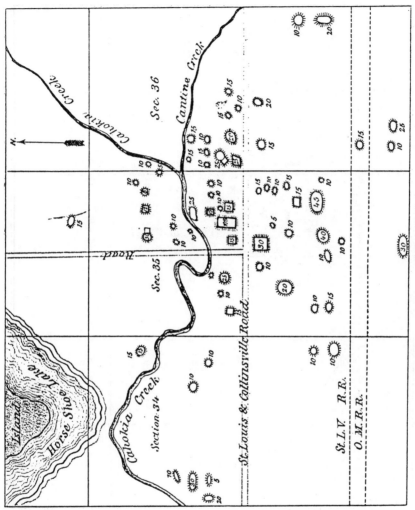

Figure 29. The McAdams 1882 Cahokia Mounds map. Monks Mound is in the central portion, with the elevation given as 108 feet (McAdams 1882).

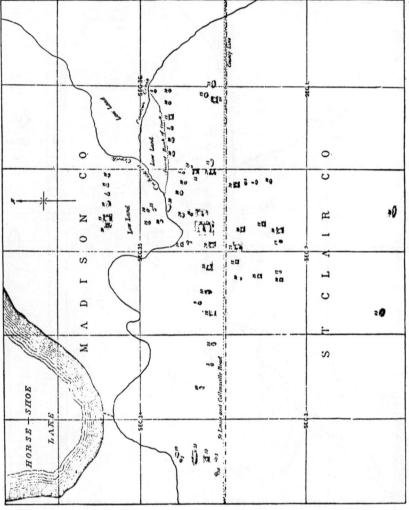

Figure 30. Cyrus Thomas's map of the Cahokia Mounds. Monks Mound is shown near the center, labeled as 100 feet high (Thomas 1894).

Figure 31. The northwest corner of Monks Mound ca. 1890. Photo courtesy Archaeological Research Laboratory, UWM

Figure 32. West side of Monks Mound ca. 1892, showing possible northwest spur

Figure 33. The west side of Monks Mound ca. 1890. Photo courtesy Archeological Research Laboratory, UWM

seems to show this ridge rather clearly. In all of the photographs, much of the west face is covered with timber.

In 1906, Cyrus Peterson and Clark McAdams, the son of William McAdams, privately published a map of the Cahokia Mounds (Figure 34) that was reproduced in Throop (1928). This is essentially a reworking of the William McAdams map, but shows Monks Mound much more accurately with a representation of the four terraces and hachures for the slopes. The better detail could reflect the earlier McAdams survey of the mound, the notes for which remained in the family (Fowler n.d.:79).

A series of photographs taken in 1914, now in the possession of the Cahokia Mounds Museum Society, show a moderately forested Monks Mound from various angles (Figures 35 through 37). Views from the north and west are not conclusive, but the long spur appears to be gone.

In 1916 the Ramey family privately commissioned a map of the area (Figure 38). The shape of Monks Mound is quite generalized, showing no second terrace, virtually no first terrace, and two rather exaggerated lobes on the east. Furthermore, extremely poor correlation with later maps, the accuracy of which are known, is evident when features are scaled from common points, such as U. S. Survey Claim boundaries. Even the Ramey structures are not placed with any degree of accuracy relative to one another and the mound.

In the 1920s Warren K. Moorehead of the University of Illinois published a series of maps of the area, but they are all more or less reliable copies of Patrick, with information concerning other mounds added. They are very valuable for Cahokia research in general, but not relevant to the study of Monks Mound, since we have the original from which they were copied.

The Modern Era

In 1922 Lieutenants Goddard and Ramey of the U. S. Army Air Service flew over the Cahokia Mounds and made the first aerial photographs of the area (see Figures 39 and 40). They are very clear low obliques. They show the mound heavily forested on the slopes but clear on the terraces. They are also a good source for the locations of modern structures.

The Goddard-Ramey photographs appear in Crook (1922) along with ground photos taken by Crook himself. In one of these, Fred Ramey stands at the northwest corner of Monks Mound; clearly absent is the spur that Patrick showed at this location (Figure 41).

The first vertical air photos of the area were flown by Colonel Dache-Reeves of the Army Air Service in 1933. These are of very good

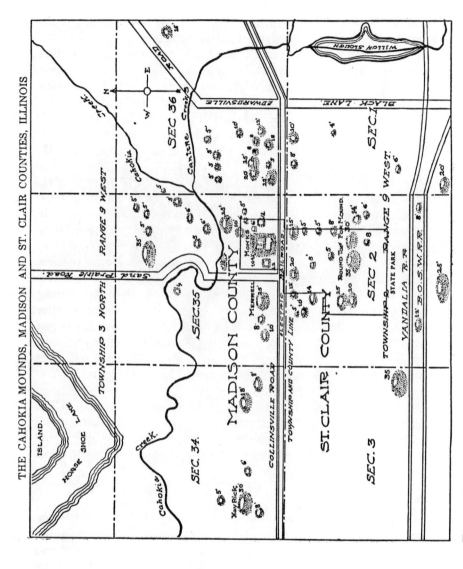

Figure 34. The Peterson-McAdams map (Throop 1928)

Figure 35. The Ramey house, built in the 1860s at the northwest corner of Monks Mound, photographed in 1914. Photo courtesy Cahokia Mounds State Historic Site

Figure 36. Monks Mound from the northeast in 1914. Photo courtesy Cahokia Mounds State Historic Site

Figure 37. Monks Mound from the north in 1914. Photo courtesy Cahokia Mounds State Historic Site

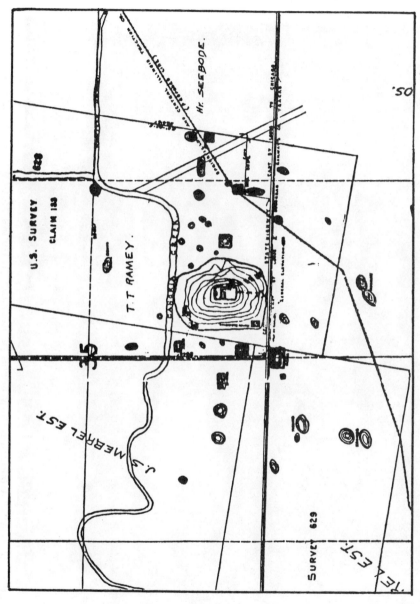

Figure 38. The Ramey family map (Fowler n.d.). Courtesy Archeological Research Laboratory, UWM

Figure 39. A 1922 Goddard-Ramey aerial photograph of Monks Mound (Crook 1922)

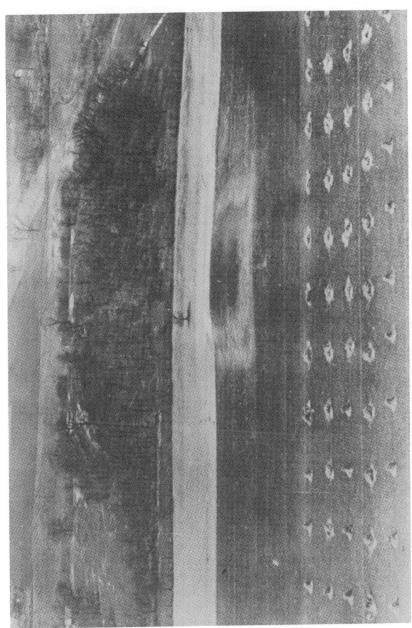

Figure 40. Another Goddard-Ramey of Monks Mound, this time from the east (Crook 1922)

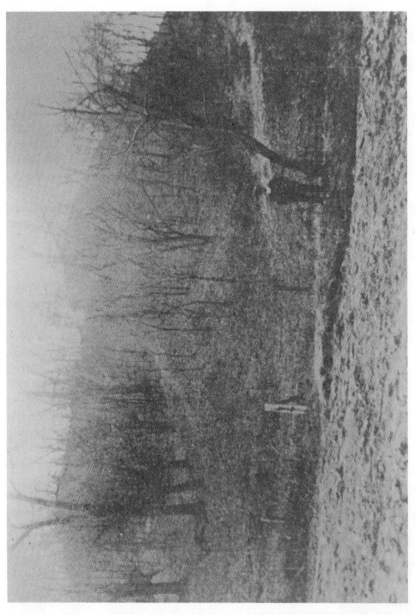

Figure 41. Fred Ramey standing at the northwest corner of Monks Mound (Crook 1922)

quality—and very important—since they were done before any major urban expansion (Figure 42).

The first good cartographic depiction of Monks Mound since Patrick appeared in a 1935 series USGS Monks Mound Quadrangle (Figure 43). Monks Mound is depicted very faithfully in 10-foot contours. It is the first map showing no prominent ridge at the northwest corner.

In 1978 the University of Wisconsin-Milwaukee compiled a map of the Cahokia area using the 1930 and 1931 field notes for the 1935 USGS map, resulting in another good contemporary view (Figure 44).

Subsequent to the 1935 series, USGS maps reverted to a more generalized depiction of Monks Mound, probably related to the increasing reliance on aerial photogrammetry.

In the 1960s the construction of interstate highways spurred the first truly intensive archaeological study of the mounds. Several detailed maps of Monks Mound were made as a result.

In 1964 a ground survey of the first terrace and the third and fourth terraces was made. It was carried out under the direction of Charles Bareis and James Porter, working on the Monks Mound Project under the auspices of the Illinois Archaeological Survey (IAS). Figure 45 shows a compiled interpolation of the two resulting maps.

In 1966 two photogrammetric maps were made: one by Lockwood Mapping, Inc., for the University of Wisconsin-Milwaukee (Figure 46), and the other by Surdex Corp., for Washington University (Figure 47). A comparison of these maps reveals a discrepancy of about a half a meter on the more or less level terraces, with good agreement on the slopes. This is apparently the result of a discrepancy between the benchmarks used in the surveys, reinforced by the lack of good resolution in photogrammetric mapping on relatively level surfaces. The Washington University map has better agreement with ground surveys, and does not show extraneous features such as archaeological excavations and the attendant back dirt piles. For this reason, it is a good choice for an overall representation of Monks Mound before the major slumping episodes of the 1980s.

In 1968 Elizabeth Benchley had a ground survey conducted for the first terrace area in connection with her work there (Figure 48). A comparison of this map with Bareis's 1964 map shows the extent to which archaeological excavation can alter the surface topography (Figure 49).

In 1984 Flagg & Associates, an Edwardsville, Illinois, surveying firm, was commissioned to do a ground survey of the entire mound in connection with the slumping on the east face that year; and in the winter of 1985, Southern Illinois University at Edwardsville (SIUE) conducted a ground survey of the second terrace area in

Figure 42. One of the Dache-Reeves aerial photographs of 1933. Monks Mound is in the lower left quadrant. Photo courtesy Cahokia Mounds State Historic Site

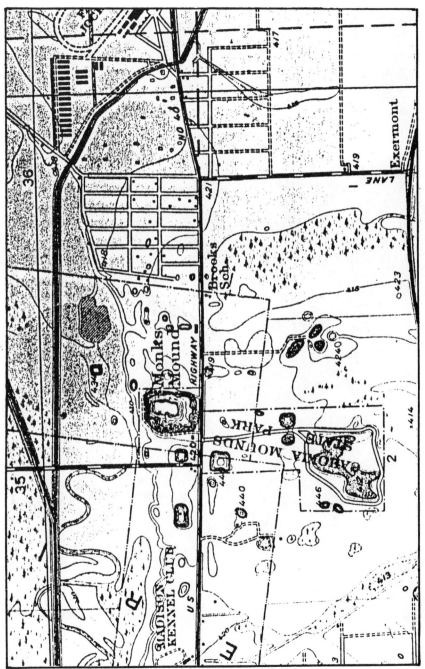

Figure 43. Detail from the 1935 series USGS 7.5' Monks Mound Quadrangle

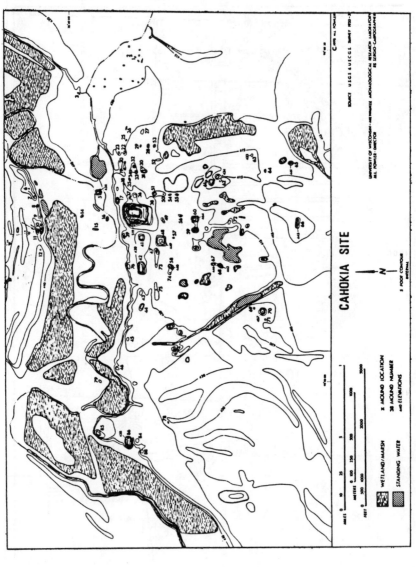

Figure 44. The University of Wisconsin-Milwaukee map compiled from the 1930 and 1931 USGS field notes (Fowler n.d.). Courtesy Melvin L. Fowler

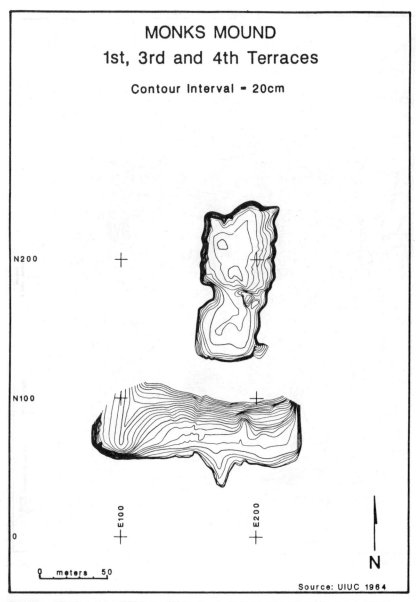

Figure 45. A compiled interpolation of the 1964 University of Illinois
maps of the first and the third and fourth terraces

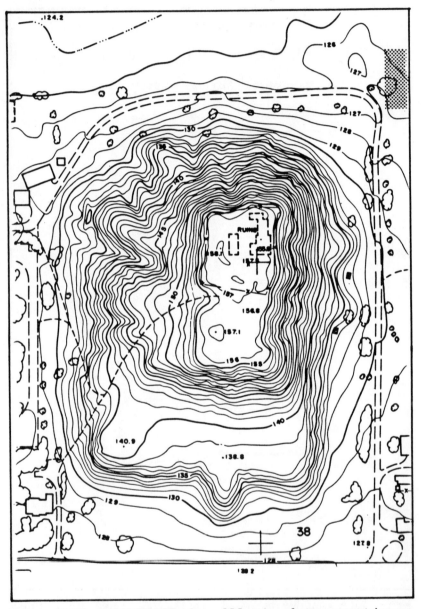

Figure 46. The 1966 UW-M/Lockwood Mapping photogrammetric map of Monks Mound (Fowler n.d.). Courtesy Melvin L. Fowler

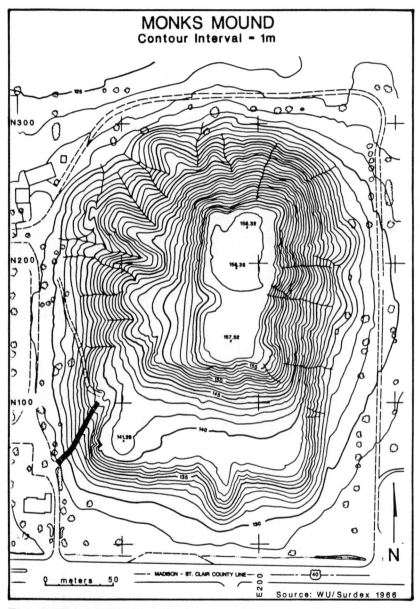

Figure 47. A metric interpolation of the WU/Surdex photogrammetric map of Monks Mound in 1966

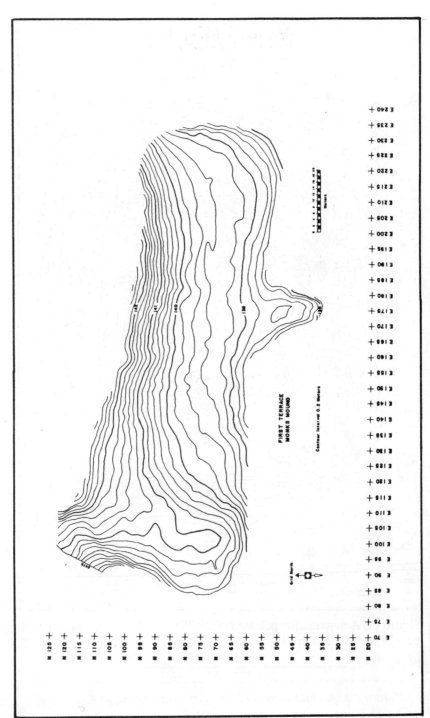

Figure 48. The UWM map of the first terrace. Courtesy Archeological Research Laboratory, UWM

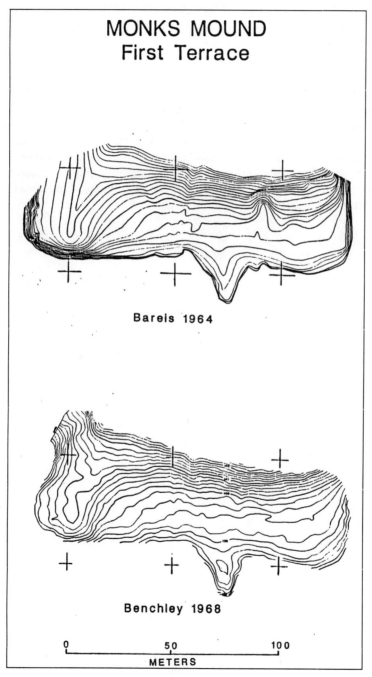

Figure 49. A comparison of two first terrace maps

connection with the slope failure there. A composite was made by SIUE of a metric interpolation of the Flagg map and the second terrace slump area (Figure 50).

All of the maps since 1964 were interpolated where required to reflect either a one-meter or twenty-centimeter contour interval and photographically reduced to the same scale for ease of comparison. Each has its strengths and weaknesses, but in general, although the photogrammetric maps are useful for an idea of the general topography of Monks Mound, the maps based on ground survey provide the most reliability where specific features are concerned. However there are no pre-slump ground surveys of the steeply sloping sections of the mound, making interpretation of earth movement in these areas difficult.

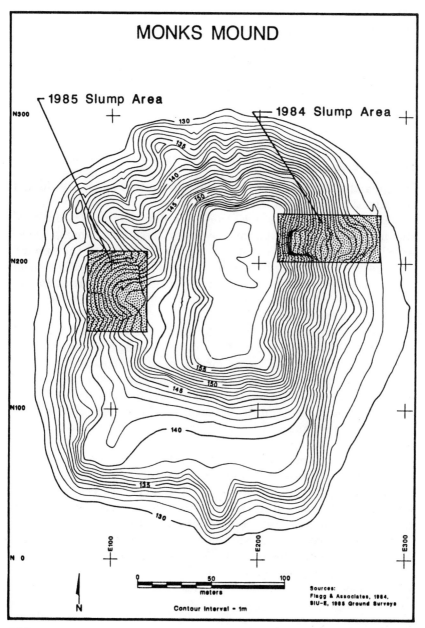

Figure 50. A composite of an interpolation of the 1984 Flagg &
Associates map and the 1985 SIUE second terrace map, showing
slump areas

Chapter 5.
The Archaeological Record

Background

In using the term "archaeology" in the context of Monks Mound investigations, one must include some activities not normally covered under that rubric, since they yielded early students of the mound the only tangible evidence they had. Among these activities are Hill's excavations on the summit of the mound preparatory to building his house, the well he subsequently dug on the second terrace, the access road he excavated from the bottom of the mound to the summit, and the tunnel Ramey began into the north face of the mound and abandoned.

Eye-witness accounts of the material uncovered during these activities provided the first data base for the testing of theories; often, however, the same data served for proponents of opposite points of view. As previously noted, early accounts and representations of these accounts were not subject to the kind of rigor one might wish for. In all cases, though, the significant feature of the accounts is that they concern cultural material from within the mound that was relevant to the debate concerning the origin of the mound. In the case of the well, cultural material was reported at the level of the surrounding plain, and it continues to provide us with information, although of a different kind. Since its present location with respect to the configuration of the second terrace lobes is known, some guesses about the previous shape of this terrace may be made.

In a more recent context, the mapping activities of Patrick, McAdams, Thomas, Bushnell, and others constituted the beginnings of the modern archaeological record. The remainder of this chapter will be concerned with intrusive activities into the mound in the twentieth century.

Early General Investigations

The first specific mention of intentional archaeological excavations in this century refers to events in 1914-16:

> Six years ago [A. R. Crook] was permitted to collect

samples of soil from Monks' mound with a two inch
auger which was sunk twenty-five feet down from the
top. . . . At another time he collected soils from holes
made with a spade and posthole digger in the north
face (Crook 1922:5).

The specific locations of the boring and the holes are not given.
Moorehead, quoting from a paper presented by Crook at the December
1914 meetings of the Geological Society of America, numbers the holes
Crook made in the north face at twenty-five (Moorehead 1928:115).
At the time he made the tests, Crook thought his evidence favored
the idea that the mound was natural and only changed his mind when
Moorehead and Leighton's excavation of James Ramey Mound (#3)
in 1921 showed similar stratification and clear proof of artificial
origin.

Moorehead and Leighton collaborated on a number of excavations
into mounds at Cahokia, but decided against actually cutting into
Monks Mound, apparently because they found its mass and extent
too daunting. They contented themselves with a series of five auger
borings, the locations of which are given only approximately
(Moorehead 1928:137-139).

The first three borings were located roughly in a north- south line
on the fourth terrace, presumably about in the middle, beginning
"near the north end" and at fifty foot intervals to the south. Their
method was to dig a pit about three feet deep and begin the borings
at the bottom. The soil in the pit stages is described as being a
homogeneous black with bits of charcoal for pits 1 and 2, with pit
3 containing "dark soil with small chips of brick in the top and charcoal fragments below, changing to dirty silty sand in the bottom."
(Moorehead 1928:138). The borings were done with a 1.25 inch auger,
which extended a distance of 17.5 feet for a total depth of 20.5 feet.
The descriptions of the soils taken from the borings are rather sketchy
and show little correlation with later coring and excavation. In the
southernmost two of the three borings on the fourth terrace,
Moorehead reports hitting a layer of sticky black gumbo about 18.5
feet, or 5.6 meters, down. At about this level, other borers report sandy
to clayey basket loading (Reed, Bennett, and Porter 1968; McGimsey
and Wiant 1984).

The remaining two borings were made on the east slope of the
mound about even with the northernmost of the borings on the fourth
terrace. The first of these was done by digging a pit on the slope, to
an elevation about 16 feet below the surface at boring 1, forming a
4-foot by 4-foot "step" in the slope. The description of the excavated
soils is extremely vague; the boring hit a gumbo layer about 5 meters

below the slope surface. The last boring was made in a similar fashion 11 feet below the previous one; the boring revealed 16 feet of the gumbo clay. Later trenches (McGimsey and Wiant 1984:48-49) in the same area show similarities with these observations, although in profile basket loading is evident in the black clayey soil. None of Moorehead and Leighton's borings go deep enough for comparison to later work that generated hypotheses concerning the stages in the construction of the mound (see below).

Fourth Terrace, First Phase

Following the work of Moorehead and Leighton, there were no intrusive investigations of Monks Mound until the 1960s. In 1964 Nelson Reed organized the Monks Mound project under the auspices of the Illinois Archaeological Survey (IAS) for the purpose of uncovering the hypothesized temple on the fourth terrace. The aim was to generate public interest to facilitate fund raising for land acquisition; a flurry of highway construction and other development activity at about this time renewed concerns for the preservation of parts of the Cahokia site outside of State control.

James W. Porter and Charles Bareis directed the excavations on the fourth terrace. A series of unconnected test units were dug to depths ranging from 1.50 to 3.50 meters below the surface; a great deal of cultural activity, both prehistoric and historic, was encountered. The remains of a farm house and its associated trash pits were uncovered at about the interface between the third and fourth terraces, generally thought to be Hill's, but possibly Ramey's (Fowler n.d.:3). If it was Hill's house, then it is too far back to have effected the removal of the secondary mound at the southeast corner. Other findings included some minor wall trenches and a large post pit near the center of the fourth terrace.

The excavations continued in 1965 under Washington University (WU) with Reed and J.W. Bennett as directors and Porter continuing as field director. The extent of excavation was increased by about fifty percent.

The Reed, Bennett, and Porter Cores

Despite those excavations some basic questions remained unanswered. In the fall of 1965 the National Science Foundation (NSF) funded a program of deep cores into the mound. In 1966 a test trench was dug so that one of its profiles contained one of the previously taken cores; it was designed to check the validity of conclusions made based on the cores (Reed, Bennett, and Porter 1968). In all nine cores were done, with one each on the first and second terraces and the remainder on the third and fourth terraces. Cores 3 inches in diameter were taken, to varying depths, with four penetrating the pre-mound surface.

The seven cores on the summit of the mound yielded evidence leading to a hypothesis of how the mound was constructed. The researchers noted occasional bands of limonite, a hydrated ferric oxide, associated with some of the distinct soil changes in their cores. Limonite can form on the surfaces of exposed soils composed of sediments with a high iron content, such as some of the Cahokia sediments, or it can percolate down in solution and precipitate at any soil boundary, even between basket loads. Reed, Bennett, and Porter proposed that where these limonite bands occur at the same or nearly the same levels in three or more cores, they have formed on previous mound surfaces that had remained exposed for a significant period of time; or, put another way, they corresponded to construction stages. Comparison of Boring 1 (Reed, Bennett, and Porter designation) with the profile of the test trench had the tendency of confirming this (Figure 51), although examination of some of the actual core profiles, on file at the Illinois State Museum, reveals somewhat less clarity than indicated in Reed, Bennett, and Porter's 1968 report.

However, given the assumptions of the investigators, the evidence indicates 14 more or less discrete construction stages. These can be reduced to eight major stages, each of which may be construed as the morphology of Monks Mound at a given time.

The base of the mound is at around 30.5 meters below the surface of the fourth terrace, or a sea level elevation of about 127.5 meters. On this surface, a small platform of black clay was built to an elevation of about 134.0, or about 6.5 meters high. No evidence of the characteristic clay fill of this mound was found under the southern part of the third terrace or the northern part of the fourth terrace, although some burned areas and bone were evident at this level near the north edge. The east-west extent is not known since the applicable borings were not deep enough to encounter this level.

Subsequently, the height of the foundation mound was raised about two meters to an elevation of about 136.0; if the horizontal extent was also increased, it was not sufficient to be picked up by the next nearest cores. But a later core (see below) does show evidence of east-west expansion at this stage.

The next major stage occurs at about 139.0 and is found roughly co-extensive with the fourth terrace, with no evidence south of it. At an elevation of about 142.0, the whole is leveled off, bringing the south end even with the north, and apparently establishing the final horizontal extent of the top, both north-south and east-west. Then at

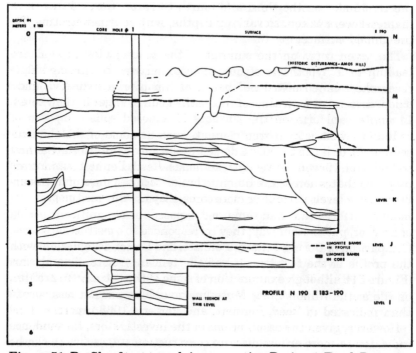

Figure 51. Profile of test trench incorporating Boring 1 (Reed, Bennett and Porter 1968). Reproduced by permission of the Society for American Archeology from American Antiquity 33:2 (1968)

about 150.5, another massive stage is found, raising the level everywhere, but considerably higher under the fourth terrace. The next major stage raises the whole to a level 154.0, and the final stage is the present two-terrace surface.

Analysis of the foregoing reveals a pattern of alternating single-level and bi-level construction; every other stage raises the level under the fourth terrace, with each succeeding stage raising the whole to a single level (Figure 52).

Radiocarbon dates from the cores suggest that Monks Mound was begun about A.D. 900, and finished about A.D. 1150 (Reed, Bennett, and Porter 1968:144-145). With the excavations on the summit and the soil borings just described, a picture of the main mass of the mound began to emerge, but little was known about the periphery.

The First and Third Terrace Interface

Along with his work on the third terrace Charles Bareis also conducted excavations at the interface between the first and third terraces for the University of Illinois from 1964 through 1972 (Figure 53) (Bareis 1975a). During the summer 1964 season he uncovered a series of step-like plateaus rising toward the third terrace. Each plateau was constructed of a mottled, yellow-brown sand and deliberately capped with a dark brown silty clay. Beneath the lowest of these plateaus and toward the south edge, he discovered a mound-like feature, composed of a heavy, dark blue-gray clay, later hypothesized to function as a buttress.

In the midst of these excavations, a trench being dug for a pipeline at the base of the west side of the mound revealed evidence of a prehistoric feature some 50 centimeters below the surface. It was subsequently judged to be a house of the late Moorehead phase (ca. A.D. 1250). An area five meters by two meters was excavated to define this feature (Bareis n.d.). The location and depth of this feature figures in later arguments against the idea that the irregularities on the west side of the mound are caused by erosion.

It was not until 1971 that Bareis returned to continue and expand his excavations at the first and third terrace interface. In the intervening years work had begun elsewhere on Monks Mound under the direction of Melvin Fowler at the University of Wisconsin-Milwaukee: Elizabeth Benchley had begun excavations on the southwest corner of the first terrace, and Kenneth Williams began work in the east lobes area. In the meantime, Fischer was mopping up for Washington University on the fourth terrace.

Bareis's expansion focused on finding the extent and function of the features uncovered in 1964 at the first and third terrace interface.

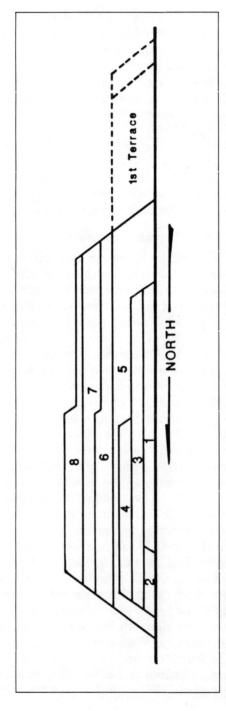

Figure 52. Schematic diagram of Monks Mound showing a possible construction sequence. The whole of the first terrace was added later.

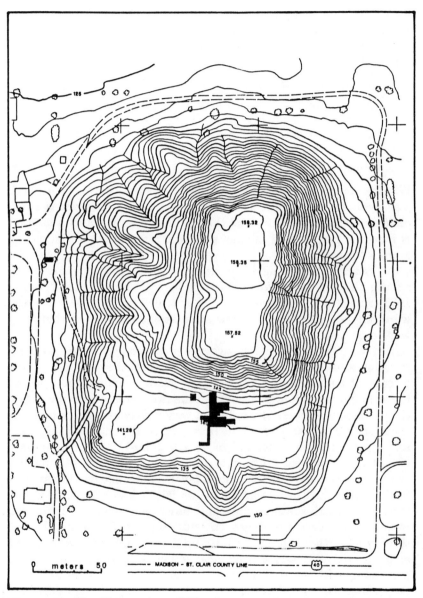

Figure 53. The University of Illinois excavations from 1964 to 1972

What he found beneath the plateaus was a series of off-set clay buttresses separated by a sandy soil fill, the first suggestion that a kind of structural engineering was employed in the construction of the mound:

> Interfill areas composed of different soils would provide good drainage and might give stability as opposed to one solid mass of clay. . . . The plateaus would cover the clay surfaces preventing excessive baking and cracking, particularly after periods of heavy rainfall (Bareis 1975a:10).

Whether or not the plateaus were used as steps, Bareis continued, was open to conjecture. The notion of building buttresses some distance from the mound, and then filling in between as a method of increasing the size of the mound would recur in other contexts at Monks Mound.

In 1972 Bareis continued and expanded his excavations to clear up a few points left unresolved the season before. The evidence from the 1971 excavations had not been sufficient to determine if the buttresses were mounds or ridges; the new excavations made clear that they were mounds.

Also in 1972, the increased coverage provided by the expanded excavation allowed measurements of the slope on the face of the third terrace. It became evident that, if one were to extend the slope as it was found at the interface between the two terraces until it reached the pre-mound surface, it would end very nearly at the north end of the south ramp that leads to the first terrace. Bareis concluded that, sometime before the Stirling Phase (A. D. 1050-1150), the main part of Monks Mound was built up to an elevation of about 149 meters, or about 21.3 meters above ground level. This stage would have extended north and south about 70 meters, with a lower third and fourth terrace. Its north-south profile would have been roughly trapezoidal, with a lower version of the south ramp in place. Subsequently, the third and fourth terraces were built up to their present elevation and an additional 30 meters was extended to the south, possibly beginning and ending with the Stirling Phase (Bareis, personal communication). Sometime after this, the first terrace and the upper part of the south ramp were constructed, possibly to act as a buttress. This model is consistent with the findings of other researchers; Reed, Bennett, and Porter (1968:146) report no evidence of the limonite bands they used to define their construction stages in the one boring they made into the first terrace at the southwest corner. They conclude that it could have been built all in one stage. The dates from Benchley's excavations at this site from 1968 through 1971 are all rather late, ranging from A.D. 1100 to A.D. 1300 (Benchley 1975:17).

One of the most significant implications of Bareis's work is that there is strong evidence that the various stages and construction sequences were carefully planned and engineered; it was not just a matter of throwing up a pile of dirt and adding to it as the spirit moved. What appeared to be fragments of wall trenches proved, with the 1972 expansions, to be the remains of fences constructed east-west across the face of the mound after completion of the plateaus. They were erected before the completion of the first terrace at the point where the first terrace would ultimately intersect the slope of the third terrace. Add to this the different soil requirements of the buttresses and infill, some of which may have required stockpiling in advance of actual construction, and

> we can infer that a group, perhaps a class, of individuals with a specialized knowledge of soils (soils or mound engineers) were responsible for directing construction of the mound (Bareis 1975b:13).

The First Terrace Secondary Mound

Benchley's work at the southwest corner of the first terrace (Figure 54) was in connection with Fowler's hypothesis that a large marker post would be found there, under the small rise at the corner. It would, he claimed, correspond to one he had found earlier on Mound 72. Fowler had projected a line through that post, the southwest corner of the first terrace, and one of the mounds in the Kunneman group, and proposed it as a possible baseline for the layout of the entire mound complex. He predicted the post would be at N70 E100 on the Cahokia Master Grid system, based on the intersection of his baseline and another line drawn between two ridge-top mounds to the east and west of Monks Mound; Fowler had hypothesized that ridge-top mounds functioned partly as boundary monuments (Fowler 1969:19).

Benchley excavated a considerable portion of the small rise during the field seasons of 1968, 1969, and 1971. She found a small rectangular secondary mound at the corner of the first terrace, with its dimensions obscured by erosion and deliberate soil deposition.

Underlying the secondary mound were two large structures, very clearly definable, and possibly two more, centering on a plaza around N70 E100, Fowler's baseline point; Benchley designates the whole as a kind of temple complex.

The easternmost structure of the complex was a large basin with rounded corners; its wall trenches were set in about 20 centimeters from the edges of the basin. Only part of the structure was uncovered,

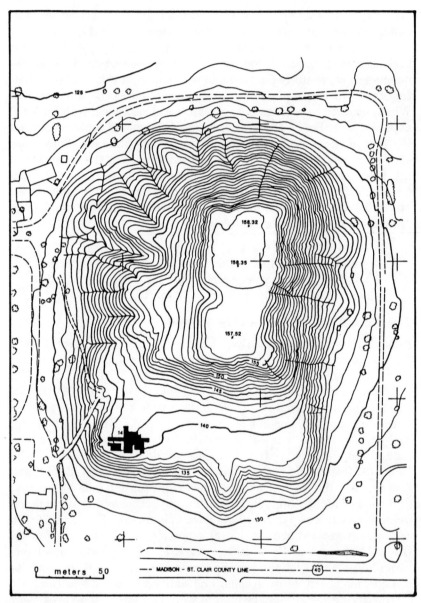

Figure 54. The University of Wisconsin-Milwaukee first terrace excavations

but there was a small crematory basin which, if it were at the center of the structure, would give it a diameter of about 20 meters. A radiocarbon sample yielded a date of A.D. 1260 plus or minus 50 years, but an archaeomagnetic sample put the date at around A.D. 1150, much more in line with its ceramics and with the other burned structure with which it is stratigraphically contemporaneous. The structure was burned *in situ* and some material removed after burning.

The southernmost structure, with a radiocarbon date of around A.D. 1110 plus or minus 55 years, was a rectangular or square shallow basin with wall trenches; its extent is not known because only one corner of it was excavated. This structure was also burned *in situ*; it appears to be partially eroded away at the edge of the first terrace.

Cultural activity continued at this location subsequent to the burning of the two structures. There is evidence of either wall trench structures or stockade walls; rodent and other disturbances severely hampered interpretation, but the ceramic association was primarily of a type called Ramey Incised, which relates to the Stirling-Moorehead Phase. In addition, apparently isolated fire pits were found, possibly "eternal fires" (Benchley n.d.:7).

There is no question that this was already an important location. Although no large posts were found at this level, there was a series of pits at Fowler's point N70 E100.

The next phase at the southwest corner involved the construction of the small mound, an event which happened fairly rapidly, possibly within 40 to 80 years (Benchley 1974:159). The construction began with an initial mound about one meter high, covering a base of about 12 by 12 meters and rising to a summit of about 10 by 10 meters. Through nine distinct stages a final platform of 24 by 26 meters at the base, and 20 by 20 meters at the 1.4 meter high summit was reached (Benchley 1974:136). The stages occurred primarily in eastward accretions, with some northward expansion as well. Possible westward expansion could not be verified due to the erosion of the first terrace. The mound was composed largely of light-colored sandy loess; the stages were identified by slight differences in the composition, with some stages composed of alternating thin bands of sand and clay. Although the surfaces of the stages were hard-packed, they were of the same material as the rest of the stage. Some water-deposited silt at the base of the mound suggests the passage of brief periods of time between stages, perhaps to allow the consolidation of the previous stage. Given this and the thickness of the siltation layers found under the east lobes, there is a possibility that there was deliberate application of water to mound surfaces in order to speed compaction.

On the east face of the small mound was a ramp-like structure, slightly south of center. In comparing the topographic map of Monks Mound commisioned by UWM (Figure 46) to the Patrick map (Figure 18), Benchley (n.d.:9) concludes that significant erosion of the first terrace has occurred since 1876 and attributes the displacement of the ramp to that erosion. Unquestionably erosion has occurred on the first terrace, but it is imprudent to assign the time and extent of it on the basis of the comparison of two such different types of maps. The corroborative evidence of the shallowness of the historic burial atop the small mound (50 centimeters) as opposed to deeper contemporaneous burials (1 meter) nearer the center of the first terrace does not seem to bear directly on the question of changes in the southward extent of the terrace.

The excavations into the small mound revealed two apparent construction techniques. The first involved dumping fill next to the mound on the side to be expanded, and adding to it until the desired elevation was reached; the second involved dumping fill well away from the face of the mound, and filling in between. This latter method recalls Bareis's system of buttresses and may also be exemplified in the east lobes area (see below). Radiocarbon, archaeomagnetic, and ceramic dates overlap with those beneath the mound suggesting it was built in late Moorehead or early Sand Prairie times (ca. A.D.1250). Several large post molds were found on the eastern slopes of the various small mound stages, including a series of superimposed posts at Fowler's baseline point of N70 E100, although these latter were considerably smaller than the post at Mound 72. The final stage of the completed mound is characterized by large structures at the summit, single posts, and a series of posts in an arc on the eastern slope.

The last deposition in this area consists of a large amount of dark fill containing animal bones and general refuse. The pottery is late, from Sand Prairie times (e.g. Wells Incised). This period saw the softening of the edges of the mound, and the beginning of a possible ramp to the second terrace. There was a great deal of activity to the north and northeast of the mound, including fires, structures, pits, and a great deal of refuse.

Several historic burials and structures to the east uncovered both by Benchley and Bareis led them to conclude that the first terrace was the site of a Cahokian Indian village, ca. A.D. 1735 to 1752, and an accompanying French mission, designated the River L'Abbe Mission by Walthall and Benchley (1987).

The Fourth Terrace Second Phase and the South Ramp

Washington University continued its work through 1972 on the third and fourth terraces and the south ramp (Figure 55). In 1970 Glen Freimuth and Lawrence Conrad replaced Porter as field directors. Reed decided to strip the top 70 centimeters from the surface of the fourth terrace in 5-meter blocks, because no features were found in the top 90 centimeters in all of the previous excavations (Reed personal communication). This revealed the extent of a large wall trench structure. The trenches that remained covered half the terrace; the north and south wall trenches could not be found, due to erosion.

In 1971 Fred Fischer took over as field director. He re-examined some of the earlier data and extended the excavation.

The excavations on the summit revealed that it had been, as expected, an important location; an immense structure had stood there, possibly surrounded by a stockade. Several enormous post pits were found as well. The structure covered an area of about 537.37 square meters and was supported in the center by six massive support posts; since no indications of domestic activity in the form of artifactual debris were found, it may be assumed the structure was of ceremonial function (Fischer n.d.:95). While the structure was apparently still in use, construction activities on the remainder of the fourth terrace continued, with several episodes of uneven filling and one case of a small terrace-like addition to the east side. In addition to the large structure, two smaller ones of unknown function were also uncovered.

The construction activities continued through two more surface configurations. Some time during the Moorehead Phase, however, emphasis appeared to shift to the first terrace.

Also in 1971 Ted Lotz excavated for Washington University in the area of the south ramp to the first terrace and discovered a pattern of posts suggestive of wooden steps up the ramp. This evidence was used as the basis of the reconstruction of steps up the ramp by Cahokia Mounds State Historic Site personnel.

The East Lobes

Other activity taking place on Monks Mound in 1971 included excavations at the more southern of the two lobe-like projections on the east face of the mound by Williams for UW-M (Williams 1975) (Figure 56).

His method was to excavate intersecting trenches to determine whether the lobes were deliberate construction features. A great deal was learned as a result of these excavations, but the findings were not necessarily conclusive.

The earliest occupation in the east lobes area was domestic, characterized by a dense concentration of house and pit features on the pre-mound level. It dates from the Late Woodland Patrick phase

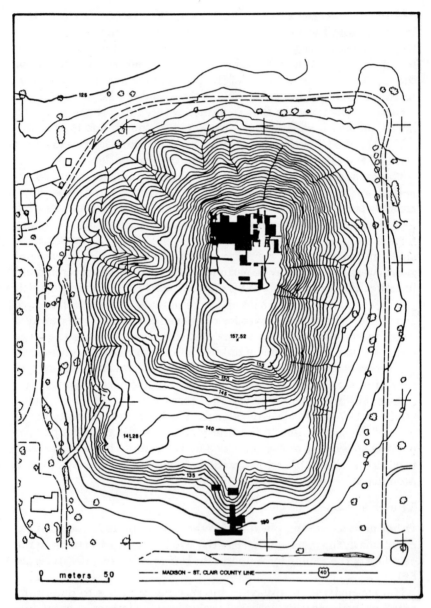

Figure 55. Washington University excavations, 1964 through 1972

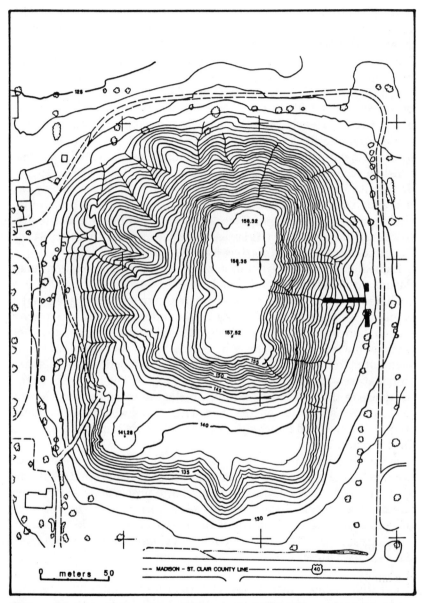

Figure 56. The University of Wisconsin-Milwaukee east lobes
excavations

(A.D. 600-800) immediately prior to the emergence of the Mississippian culture. This was overlain by a 1.5-meter thick zone of highly stratified water-borne siltation, apparently from erosion of Monks Mound construction stages. Since the siltation does not occur at nearby locations (Williams 1975:23), alluvial depositions are unlikely.

Judging from the ceramics in this layer, silt was deposited over a period of about 250 years, from about A.D. 900 (Merrell phase) to about A.D. 1150 (early Moorehead phase)—during the construction of the mound (see Reed, Bennett, and Porter 1968:144-145). Since the siltation apparently stopped once the mound was completed, one must consider the possibility that the erosion was due either to the deliberate application of water or because no tightly packed clay cap was added during each construction phase. At the bottom of the siltation layer was evidence of a stockade wall, reminiscent of the prolific fence-building on the first terrace and especially the fence at the first and third terrace interface reported by Bareis.

Immediately above the siltation zone were several occupation zones dating to Moorehead and Sand Prairie times (A.D. 1150-1500). Included in the latter is a ridge or buttress-like feature where human remains were found. Williams's initial interpretation was that a trench had been dug parallelling Monks Mound and a burial or burials placed inside. The whole was then backfilled and supplemented to form the ridge, which buttressed a deliberate construction feature—the east lobes (Williams 1975:23). The last level in the sequence is the lobe itself, exhibiting clear signs of basket loading; no dates are available for this zone. This model would have analogs in both Bareis's and Benchley's interpretations of construction on the first terrace.

Since the publication of this interpretation, however, events have occurred that have caused the excavator to change his mind (Williams n.d.). In 1984 a slope failure of fairly large proportions occurred on the more northern of the two east lobes, resulting in the shearing off and slumping of a portion of the east face at that location.

As a result, the Illinois Department of Conservation (IDOC) funded two investigations. John Mathes and Associates, an Illinois geotechnical engineering firm, studied ways of controlling the slump. The Illinois State Museum Society was hired to interpret the area archaeologically (McGimsey and Wiant 1984). Toward this end, the archaeologists examined five solid cores taken at various points by Mathes, six backhoe trenches put in at the immediate area of the slumpage and the site of a previous slump on the north face, and the scarp formed by the break on the east face (Figure 57).

Their profile of the toe of the slump showed some strong similarities

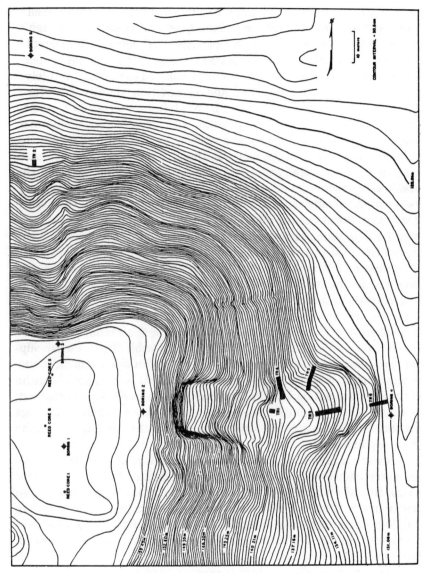

Figure 57. The Illinois State Museum slump investigations (McGimsey and Wiant 1984)

to Williams's profiles a few meters to the south (Figures 58 and 59). Specifically, the ridge-like morphology of McGimsey and Wiant's Zones T6-D & E recalled Williams's Feature 285, formerly interpreted as a buttress. This caused Williams to re-interpret his data.

Some of the basket loads in the lobe fill had exhibited tumbling, as if by contact with a failure plane. In addition, the fill of Feature 285 had always been similar to the overlying material; in fact, the difference was ". . . somewhat difficult to discern . . ." (Williams n.d.:57), the presence or absence of clear basket loading being the primary determinant. The more southern of the east lobes was now regarded as being totally the result of slumping. The human remains, previously considered a burial, were now conjectured to have been swept from the surface of a small platform mound by the relentless advance of the slumping mound face. The eastern meter or so of this platform had been uncovered in one of the trenches. A mortuary structure of some type was hypothesized for the platform mound to explain the presence of the skeleton. Although no evidence of such a structure was found and little of the mound itself was uncovered, this is not inconsistent with the hypothesis.

There are, however, some problems with this model, too. In McGimsey and Wiant's profile of the known toe of a slump, the separation between Zones T6-D and T6-E is unmistakable: T6-D is a densely compact, swirled, yellowish-brown silty clay; in other words, it exhibits intensive tumbling of basket loads; T6-E is composed largely of the same materials, but the lenticular basket loads are undisturbed over the clearly apparent shear plane, or "slickenside," as it is so designated. This is not the case with Williams's features 285 and 288, the ridge and the fill above it. Although the southern lobe does show clear evidence of tumbled basket loads, McGimsey and Wiant's slump toe is reported as being ". . . plastic, swirled, distorted, . . . very compact and stiff" (McGimsey and Wiant 1984:50), evidence of extreme forces that in the end pushed the leading edge of the slump only 60 centimeters over the previous ground surface. If Williams's version of events in the southern lobe is correct, that slump would have moved several meters horizontally.

There is no compelling reason to choose between the two interpretations of the more southern of the east lobes; McGimsey and Wiant (1984:37) report evidence in their Trench 2 of prehistoric slumping and repair episodes on the north face of Monks Mound. If slumping is to account for a significant part of the south lobe, it, too, must have occurred in prehistoric times since there was no vegetation layer evident below the lobe fill. Some combination of slumping and intentional construction may well be the answer.

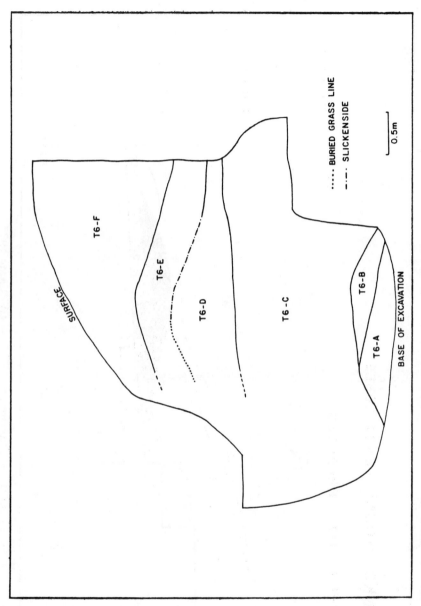

Figure 58. Profile of the toe of the 1984 slump (McGimsey and Wiant 1984)

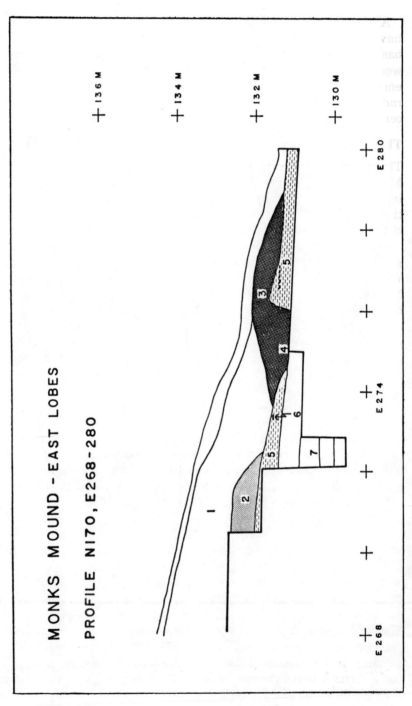

Figure 59. Profile of the toe of the southernmost east lobe (Williams 1975)

A better idea of chronology in relation to the rest of the mound may have proved useful, particularly in Williams's Feature 288, the basket-loaded, lobe-fill zone. The only dates for McGimsey and Wiant's work are relative and based on local stratigraphy. Apparently they encountered no cultural material in their excavations. There are no radiocarbon dates, no archaeomagnetic dates, and no diagnostic ceramics.

The McGimsey and Wiant Cores

The results of the cores are somewhat less problematic. Although McGimsey and Wiant disagree with Reed, Bennett, and Porter regarding their interpretations of their cores, there are very good correlations with most of the latter's major mound stages and distinct soil changes in the former's cores.

The disagreement is founded on two points: limonite can form on surfaces other than exposed mound surfaces, and McGimsey and Wiant found very little evidence of the limonite bands in their cores. Not much can be said about the second point, but the first point had been taken into consideration: "Those bands which appear in only one or two cores may indicate local rather than mound-wide construction, or that Indian excavations occurred at these . . . places" (Reed, Bennett, and Porter 1968:142). Limonite bands occurring consistently in several cores at the same level must be attributable to more than coincidence. However, it should be pointed out that the original core profiles used by Reed, Bennett, and Porter show a profusion of what appears to be limonite bands, and a correlation with the stylized depiction in their 1968 article is difficult, at best. This, coupled with the fact that McGimsey and Wiant were forced by circumstances to draw rather hasty profiles of their cores in the field, tends to dilute the value of a comparison of the two sets of cores.

In any case the correlations, such as they are, are there. To begin with, there is agreement on the level of the pre-mound surface at an elevation just below 128.00. Then, Reed, Bennett, and Porter's Stage A finds corroboration in McGimsey and Wiant's cores 1 and 3 (Zones 1-H and 3-I); core 2, at the eastern edge of the fourth terrace, shows no change here, but this could be an indicator that the foundation mound did not extend that far. On the other hand, Zone 2-K shows up at the level of Stage B; this stage could have expanded the mound eastward as well as vertically. Stage D, the next major stage, shows up very clearly in McGimsey and Wiant's Zones 1-G and 3-H and in a change in the middle of Zone 2-J. The tops of Zones 2-J and 3-E, and a distinct noted change in mid 1-F, correspond well to the top of Reed, Bennett, and Porter's Stage E.

The next major stage corresponds to Stages F and G, and again, McGimsey and Wiant report changes at Zones 1-E, 2-H, and 3-D. The same occurs again; combined Stages L and M correspond to Zones 1-D 2-E, and a change is noted within 3-B. That these correlations exist where construction stages are conjectured argues in favor of the hypothesis, but more evidence would be desirable.

The Second Terrace

The slope failure on the east face of Monks Mound was not the first. A slump occurred on the west face near the juncture of the first and second terraces in 1956 and another on the north face during the late 1960s (McGimsey and Wiant 1984:1). Nor was it the last.

In the late winter of 1985, the southernmost and largest of the lobes on the west side of Monks Mound—most commonly referred to as the second terrace—began to slump nearly a meter along an irregular shear plane (see Figure 60). The Illinois Historic Preservation Agency (IHPA), superceding IDOC, again engaged Mathes and Associates to examine the situation. Southern Illinois University at Edwardsville (SIUE), under the overall direction of William I. Woods, performed archaeological investigations. Among other things, it was a unique opportunity to examine the second terrace, about which much had been conjectured, but very little resolved. There was some sense of urgency since, unlike other slump episodes at the mound, this one resumed its activity during the rains of November 1985 after an apparently stable period during the dry summer months. It appears to have stabilized since then, but at the time, it was a novel situation, and no one knew what to expect.

SIUE, directed in the field by James Collins, recorded eight profiles at intervals along the scarp and excavated a six-by- four-meter test trench in the immediate vicinity of the slump (see Figure 61). As a result of these activities the archaeologists determined that the top meter or so of the second terrace was composed of three separate fill episodes, designated Units I, II, and III.

Unit I, the topmost soil stratum, was interpreted as a series of mound surfaces developed from colluvial deposition from the third and fourth terraces. There were no cultural features in this unit, which varied in thickness an average of about 0.5 meter. The ceramic sequence from this unit covers the spectrum from Emergent Mississippian through recent historic times, as to be expected, given its colluvial nature.

Unit II, a layer of relatively light-colored, coarse-textured sandy soil, terminated in a prehistoric surface intruded by Feature 1, an irregular basin which did not extend below into Unit III soils. In one

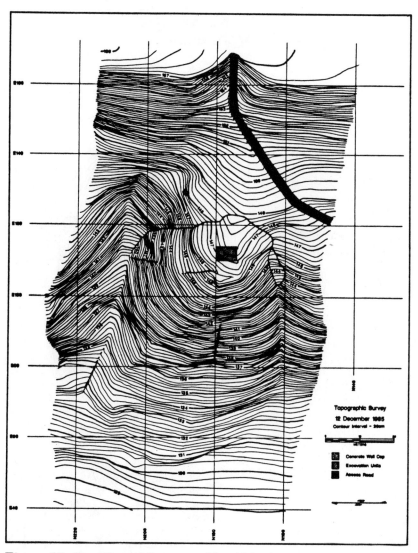

Figure 60. A section of the west side of Monks Mound, showing the
1985 slump scarp and SIUE excavation

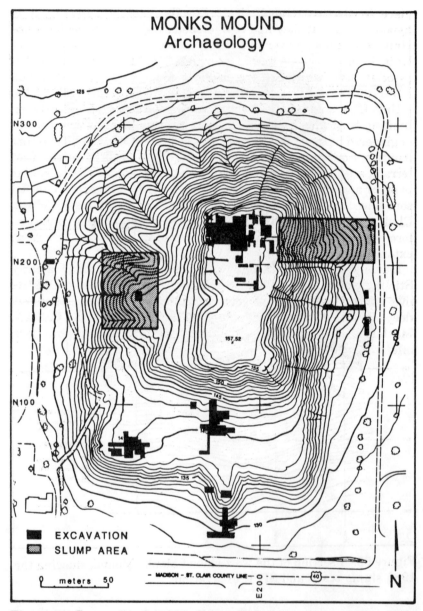

Figure 61. Composite showing all recorded excavations and the 1984 and 1985 slump areas on Monks Mound

place in the test trench, Unit II soils were not present; it is hypothesized that they had been eroded away prehistorically, since Unit I soils directly overlaid Unit III soils. The soft, loose nature of Unit II lends credence to this interpretation. Temporally, Unit II is associated with late Stirling or early Moorehead times, between A.D. 1100-1200.

Unit III, a dome-shaped zone of variegated mound fill clearly exhibiting lenticular basket loads, was interpreted as an intentional, engineered buttress to the west face of Monks Mound. Alternating bands of soil types, reminiscent of Bareis's findings on the first terrace, are clearly present, and the gross morphology appears similar to other apparent buttresses. According to the excavators, "Unit III soils have functioned and continue to function as a buttress" (Collins, Chalfant, and Holley 1986:18). There was evidence that the dome was forcing the slumpage to the north rather than to the west to a great extent.

Intrusive into this unit, dated by ceramics to the Lohmann or early Stirling phase (A.D. 1000-1100), is Feature 2, a large post pit a little over a meter in diameter and determined by probing to be 1.75 meters deep. It centers at approximately N178.5 E110.5 on the Cahokia Master Grid. No definitive interpretation of its function has been offered.

Chapter 6.
Summary And Conclusion

The foregoing evidence suggests a picture of Monks Mound as it evolved through time. The picture is in some periods sketchy, and in others, quite clear.

Naturally, given the type and scarcity of the evidence, the period of its construction and subsequent prehistoric use is the most difficult to reconstruct. There are some conclusions that can be drawn from the archaeological record, although at this point many of them are more hypothesis than theory and require additional study.

There is general agreement that construction began around A.D. 900, early in the Emergent Mississippian Period, on a site that had seen intensive occupation during the previous Late Woodland phases. McGimsey and Wiant report a radiocarbon date from the surface below the mound at about the center of the fourth terrace of about A.D. 840 plus or minus 70 years (McGimsey and Wiant 1984:Addendum), which corroborates that date. Initially a platform a little over six meters high was constructed of black clay, though probably not co-extensive horizontally with the present dimensions of the main body of the mound (that is, excluding the second and first terrace areas). How long the construction remained at this stage is not known, but probably not very long. In any event, the next addition added two meters of height and very likely increased the horizontal extent as well.

Construction proceeded through six more stages, alternating bi-level and single level additions, until the present two-terrace summit was reached sometime in the late Stirling or early Moorehead phase (ca. A.D. 1150). The length of time during and between these stages is not known.

This stage of the mound was without the first terrace apron, although the south ramp, in some form, seems to have been present. The problematic second terrace, however, was present very early on, certainly in Stirling times, and functioned as a buttress. Its addition may have been prompted by slumping on the east and north faces of the mound during the Stirling phase.

Immediately following the completion of the main body of the mound the first terrace apron was added, apparently all at once. A small (probably two meters high and 24-by-26 meters at the base) secondary mound was added at the southwest corner of the first terrace during the Moorehead phase, when focus seemed to be shifting there from the summit terraces. A similar secondary mound, a little over three meters high, was constructed at an unknown time at the southeast corner of the third terrace. One has to wonder what caused the shift of emphasis from the fourth terrace by Moorehead times. In any event, by the end of the Moorehead phase (ca. A.D. 1250) Monks Mound was essentially finished, and no additions of any significance were made.

The next 500 years or so are not well understood; archaeologically speaking, they are characterized by an increase in general refuse, particularly on the first terrace where black, loamy soil was added or developed in places. These are not clearly intentional building episodes; they could well represent concentrations of cultural debris. The Mississippian culture was apparently in decline during the earlier part of this period, and that may be reflected in what appears to be the much more mundane occupation of Monks Mound.

By the eighteenth century, Cahokia Indians had moved into the area, responding to pressure from other Illinois groups from the north. They were well established by the time the French arrived. At least between A.D. 1735 and A.D. 1752, a group of Cahokia Indians lived on the first terrace of Monks Mound, and the French had an active mission there.

Following the abandonment of the mission, which may have been the victim of an attack by a rival Tamaroa group, little is known until a small group of Trappist monks acquired the land containing the mound in 1809 and sought to establish a monastery there. There is a general consensus that their buildings were located on a smaller mound nearby, but they cultivated the level areas of the big mound, had a kitchen garden on the first terrace, and sowed wheat on the third and fourth terraces. Several contemporary accounts assert that they intended to build on the big mound, and one states that they did; but the consensus is that they did not, despite the general belief during most of the nineteenth century to the contrary. When the monastery failed in 1813, the Trappists returned to Europe, leaving little behind but the name Monks Mound. From this time forward, the mound enters a period of occasional intentional modification and an alternating pattern of forestation and denuding.

The earliest accounts indicate that trees covered the north face during the time of the monks, and following their departure, a thick growth of weeds was evident all over Monks Mound. In the 1830s,

Hill built his structures on the summit, cut his road, and dug his well, apparently leaving the sides forested, although Bodmer's drawings from this period show them bare. Both Latrobe and Flagg describe trees on the sides, and Flagg specifically mentions the size and age of the oaks. By 1841 Hill had grown fruit and shade trees on the summit.

Shortly after this period, accounts begin to appear of "recent" erosion, attributed to modern activities, but it is apparent that the described damage existed long before. A drawing from the 1870s shows the mound moderately timbered. The well on the second terrace is depicted on relatively flat ground.

Photographs from just before the turn of the century show the continued moderate tree cover; the sides appear heavily forested only on the north, and in 1903 it is reported that cattle and sheep grazed on the mound. At some time before this, a large cut was made near the northwest corner of the mound, and a brick house with outbuildings was constructed, along with a road up to the terrace above from the north.

After the turn of the century, little change is evident, with the conspicuous exception of the apparent removal of a large spur sloping to the northwest from the corner of the fourth terrace. The evidence for the spur is its clear depiction on Patrick's meticulously detailed cast-iron model from 1876 and an ambiguous 1882 reference by McAdams to a small mound in the northwest corner. Photographic evidence indicates that the spur was gone by 1922, but earlier photographs are inconclusive.

Changes since the 1920s primarily involve the removal of buildings when the area was acquired by the State of Illinois and known episodes of slumping and filling, which appear to have changed the contours of the mound rather little. Some of the recent slumping occurred before the tree removal in the 1960s, although the most conspicuous slumps occurred after.

Judging from large-scale topographic maps of the mound made in connection with archaeological investigations on Monks Mound, nearly as much change in the superficial morphology of the mound can be attributed to archaeology as to slumping.

One question that a study of this nature might be expected to resolve is whether or not the recent slumping can be attributed to recent human activities on the mound, notably the removal of trees. It does seem that the slumping coincides to some degree with tree removal, but a better correlation exists with two periods in this century of alternate drought and record rainfall (see Collins, Chalfant, and Holley 1986). The careful structural engineering of the mound appears to have been overcome somewhat by this extreme situation. Woods (personal communication) suggests that the shrinking of the component soils during water draw-down periods has caused the clay caps, which previously allowed water to run off, to crack and allow water to enter. There is also evidence that slumps and failures of various kinds occurred and were repaired prehistorically; one of the contributing factors in the extent of the modern failures could be the lack of constant "grooming".

Although the bad news is that the structure of Monks Mound seems vulnerable to climatological extremes, the good news is that it appears to stabilize quite rapidly when these extremes no longer exist. Thus, despite the long history of concern that "recent" activities were damaging the mound and would ultimately cause its complete collapse, it appears to be remarkably resistant to indirect interference; that is to say, the most obvious damage has been when parts of the mound have been intentionally altered or removed.

A general conclusion may be reached that, once the mound construction was completed sometime around A.D. 1150, its overall morphology changed very little in the 800-odd years until the present. What we see today is very like what the Mississippians abandoned when their culture disappeared.

References Cited

Anonymous
  n.d. *Madison County Road Records*, Book 2. On file, Madison County, Illinois Recorder of Deeds.

  1873 *Illustrated Encyclopedia and Atlas Map of Madison County (Illinois)*. W.R. Brink. St. Louis.

  1881 *History of St. Clair County, Illinois*. Brink, McDonough, and Company. Philadelphia.

Bareis, Charles J.
  n.d. Field map on file, Department of Anthropology, University of Illinois. Urbana.

  1975a Report of 1971 University of Illinois-Urbana Excavations at the Cahokia Site. In *Cahokia Archaeology: Field Reports*. Illinois State Museum Research Series. Papers in Anthropology, No. 3. Springfield.

  1975b Report of 1972 University of Illinois-Urbana Excavations at the Cahokia Site. In *Cahokia Archaeology: Field Reports*. Illinois State Museum Research Series. Papers in Anthropology, No. 3. Springfield.

Baum, Henry Mason
  1903 Antiquities of the United States: The Cahokia Mounds. *Records of the Past*, Vol. II. Washington, D.C.

Benchley, Elizabeth
  n.d. Excavations on the Southwest Corner of the First Terrace of Monks Mound, East St. Louis, Illinois, 1968-1969: A Summary. Unpublished manuscript on file, Department of Anthropology, University of Wisconsin-Milwaukee.

  1974 *Mississippian Secondary Mound Loci: A Comparative Functional Analysis in a Time-Space Perspective*. Ph.D. dissertation, Department of Anthropology, University of Wisconsin-Milwaukee.

1975   Summary Field Report of Excavations on the Southwest Corner of the First Terrace of Monks Mound: 1968, 1969, 1971. In *Cahokia Archaeology: Field Reports*. Illinois State Museum Research Series. Papers in Anthropology, No. 3. Springfield.

Bodmer, Karl
1834   *Karl Bodmer's America*. Joslyn Art Museum and University of Nebraska Press, 1984. Lincoln.

Boellstorff, John
1978   North American Pleistocene Stages Reconsidered in Light of Probable Pliocene-Pleistocene Continental Glaciation. In *Science*, vol. 202, no. 20.

Bowman, Isaiah
1907   *Water Resources of the East St. Louis District*. Illinois State Geological Survey Bulletin No. 5. Urbana.

Brackenridge, Henry Marie
1811   Unsigned article in *The Missouri Gazette*, January 9. St. Louis.

1813   On the Population and Tumuli of the Aborigines of North America. In a letter to Thomas Jefferson. *Transactions of the American Philosophical Society*. Philadelphia.

1814   *Views of Louisiana Together with a Journal of a Voyage up the Missouri River, in 1811*, Pittsburgh. (Modern Edition, 1962. Quadrangle Books. Chicago).

Collins, James M., Michael L. Chalfant and George R. Holley
1986   Archaeological Testing of the Slump Area on the West Face of Monks Mound, Madison County, Illinois. Unpublished report submitted to John Mathes and Associates, Inc., Columbia, Illinois. On file, Contract Archaeology Program, Southern Illinois University-Edwardsville.

Collot, Georges Victor
1826   *Voyage dans l'Amerique Septentrionale, ou Description des Pays Arroses par le Mississippi, l'Ohio, le Missouri et Autres Rivieres Affluentes*. A. Bertrand. Paris.

Crook, A.R.
1922   The Origin of the Cahokia Mounds. *Bulletin of the Illinois State Museum*. Springfield.

DeHass, Wills
    1869   Archaeology of the Mississippi Valley. *Proceedings of the American Association for the Advancement of Science. 17th Meeting Held at Chicago, Illinois, August, 1868.* Joseph Lovering. Springfield.

Featherstonhaugh, G.W.
    1844   *Excursion through the Slave States.* Vol. 1. Harper. London and New York.

Fenneman, F. E.
    1907   Stratigraphic Work in the Vicinity of East St. Louis. In *Year-Book for 1906.* Illinois State Geological Survey Bulletin No. 4. Urbana.

    1909   *Physiography of the St. Louis Area.* Illinois State Geological Survey Bulletin No. 12. Urbana.

Fischer, Fred W.
    n.d.   Recent Archaeological Investigations on the 4th Elevation of Monks Mound, Madison County, Illinois. Unpublished manuscript on file, Department of Anthropology, Washington University, St. Louis.

Flagg, Edmund
    1838   *The Far West: or, A Tour Beyond the Mountains.* Vol. 1. Harper and Brothers. New York.

Foster, John Wells
    1887   *Prehistoric Races of the United States of America.* S.C. Griggs and Company. Chicago.

Fowler, Melvin L.
    n.d.   *A History of Investigations at the Cahokia Mounds Historic Site and Atlas of Mounds and other Aboriginal Features.* In Press.

    1969   The Cahokia Site. In *Explorations into Cahokia Archaeology,* Illinois Archaeological Survey Bulletin 7. Urbana.

Fowler, Melvin L. and Robert L. Hall
    1975   Archaeological Phases at Cahokia. In *Perspectives in Cahokia Archaeology,* Illinois Archaeological Survey Bulletin 10. Urbana.

Frye, John C. and H. B. Willman
    1975   Quaternary System. In *Handbook of Illinois Stratigraphy,* Illinois State Geological Survey Bulletin 95. Urbana.

Grimm, R. E., editor
1949   *Cahokia Brought to Life*. The Greater St. Louis Archae-
        ological Society. St. Louis.

Hennepin, Louis
1698   *A New Discovery of a Vast Country in America*. M.
        Bentley, J. Tonson, H. Bontwick, T. Goodwin, and S.
        Manship. London. (Modern edition, A. C. McClure and
        Company, 1903. Chicago).

James, James A.
1928   *The Life of George Rogers Clark*. University of Chicago
        Press. Chicago.

LaTrobe, Charles Joseph
1835   *The Rambler in North America*. Vol. II. Harper and
        Brothers. New York.

Leighton, M. M., George E. Ekblaw and Leland Horberg
1948   Physiographic Divisions of Illinois. *Journal of Geology*,
        No. 56.

Long, Stephen H.
1823   Account of an Expedition from Pittsburgh to the Rocky
        Mountains Performed in the years 1819 and 1820.
        Compiled from the Notes of Maj. Long, Mr. T. Say, and
        other Gentlemen of the Party by Edwin James. In *Early
        Western Travels 1748-1846*, Vol. XIV. Reuben Gold
        Thwaites, editor. 1905. The Arthur H. Clark Company.
        Cleveland.

MacLean, John Patterson
1885   *The Mound Builders*. R. Clarke and Company.
        Cincinnati.

McAdams, William
1882   Antiquities. In *History of Madison County, Illinois*. W.R.
        Brink and Company. Edwardsville.

1887   *Records of Ancient Races in the Mississippi Valley*. C.R.
        Barns Publishing Company. St. Louis.

1895   Archaeology. In *Report of the Illinois Board of World's
        Fair Commissioners at the World's Columbian Exposi-
        tion, May 1 - October 30 1893*. Springfield.

McDermott, John Francis
1949   *Old Cahokia*. St. Louis Historical Documents Founda-
        tion. St. Louis.

McGimsey, Charles R. and Michael D. Wiant
    1984   *Limited Archaeological Investigations at Monks Mound
            (11-MS-38): Some Perspectives on its Stability, Structure
            and Age.* Illinois State Historic Preservation Office
            Studies in Illinois Archaeology, No. 1; Illinois State
            Museum Society Archaeological Research Program
            Technical Report No. 196. Springfield.

Messinger, John
    1808   Field Notes for the South Edge of Town 3 North, Range
            9 West of the 3rd Principal Meridian. In *Illinois Land
            Records, Original Field Notes,* 12:76 Illinois State Ar-
            chives. Microfiche. Springfield.

Moorehead, Warren K.
    1922   The Cahokia Mounds: A Preliminary Report. *University
            of Illinois Bulletin,* Vol. XIX, No. 35. April 24. Urbana.

    1928   The Cahokia Mounds. *University of Illinois Bulletin,* Vol.
            26, No. 4. Urbana.

Oliver, William
    1843   *Eight Months in Illinois; with Information to Immi-
            grants.* William Andrew Mitchell. Newcastle upon Tyne.
            (Modern edition, 1924, the Torch Press. Cedar Rapids,
            Iowa).

Peck, John Mason
    1834   *Gazetteer of Illinois.* R. Goudy. Jacksonville.

Peet, Stephen D.
    1891   The Great Cahokia Mound. *The American Antiquarian,*
            Vol. 13, No. 1. Chicago.

Putnam, F.W., and J.J.R. Patrick
    1880   Twelfth Annual Report of the Peabody Museum. *Reports
            of the Peabody Museum of American Archaeology and
            Ethnology in Connection with Harvard University,
            1876-79,* Vol. II. Cambridge.

Reed, Nelson A., John W. Bennett and James Warren Porter
    1968   Solid Core Drilling of Monks Mound: Technique and
            Findings. *American Antiquity,* Vol. 33, No. 2.

Reynolds, John
    1879   *My Own Times: Embracing also the History of My Life.*
            Chicago Historical Society. Chicago.

Shaw, E. W.
    1911   Extinct Lakes in Southern and Western Illinois and
            Adjacent States. In *Year-Book for 1910*. Illinois State
            Geological Survey Bulletin No. 20. Urbana.

Short, John T.
    1880   *The North Americans of Antiquity*. Harper and Brothers.
            New York.

Smith, Harlan Ingersoll
    1902   The Great American Pyramid. In *Harper's Monthly
            Magazine*, Vol. 104. New York.

Snyder, John Francis
    1909   Prehistoric Illinois. Certain Indian Mounds Technically
            Considered. *Journal of the Illinois State Historical
            Society*, Vols. 1 and 2. Springfield.

    1917   The Great Cahokia Mound. *Illinois State Historical
            Society Journal*, Vol. 10. Springfield.

Thomas, Cyrus
    1894   Report on the Mound Explorations of the Bureau of
            Ethnology. *12th Annual Report of the Bureau of
            Ethnology, 1890-91*. Washington, D.C.

Throop, Addison J.
    1928   *The Mound Builders of Illinois*. Call Printing Company.
            East St. Louis.

Titterington, Paul F.
    1938   *The Cahokia Mound Group and Its Village Site Material*.
            St. Louis.

Tonti, Henri de
    1704   *Relation of Henri de Tonti concerning the Explorations
            of LaSalle from 1678 to 1683*. The Caxton Club, 1898.
            Chicago.

Walthall, John A., and Elizabeth Benchley
    1987   *The River L'Abbe Mission*. Studies in Illinois Ar-
            chaeology No. 2. Illinois Historic Preservation Agency.
            Springfield.

Webster, Noah
    1789   Letter from Noah Webster, Esq., to the Rev. Ezra Stiles
            D.D. In *The American Museum or Universal Magazine*
            vol. VI. University Microfilms, APS 1 Reel 4. Ann Arbor.

Wild, J.C.
   1841   *The Valley of the Mississippi; Illustrated in a Series of Views.* Chambers and Knapp. St. Louis.

Williams, Kenneth
   n.d.   Final Report of Investigations at the East Lobes of Monks Mound. Unpublished manuscript on file, Department of Anthropology, University of Wisconsin-Milwaukee.

   1975   Preliminary Summation of Excavations at the East Lobes of Monks Mound. In *Cahokia Archaeology:Field Reports.* Illinois State Museum Research Series. Papers in Anthropology, No. 3. Springfield.

Willman, H.B., and John C. Frye
   1970   *Pleistocene Stratigraphy of Illinois.* Illinois State Geological Survey Bulletin 94. Urbana.

Willman, H. B., Elwood Atherton, T. C. Buschbach, Charles Collinson, John C. Frye, M. E. Hopkins, Jerry A. Lineback and Jack A. Simon
   1975   Introduction. In *Handbook of Illinois Stratigraphy,* Illinois State Geological Survey Bulletin 95. Urbana.

Worthen, A. H.
   1866   *Geological Survey of Illinois, Volume 1: Geology.* Springfield.

Yarbrough, Ronald E.
   1974   The Physiography of Metro East. *Bulletin of the Illinois Geographical Society,* Vol. XVI, No. 1.